THE COUNTRY LIFE LIBRARY OF ANTIQUES

CHAIRS

THE COUNTRY LIFE LIBRARY OF ANTIQUES

CHAIRS

Edward T. Joy

COUNTRY LIFE BOOKS

Frontispiece
X-frame chair of *c.* 1560; the upholstery is modern.
Vestry, York Minster.

Published by Country Life Books
and distributed for them by
The Hamlyn Publishing Group Limited
London · New York · Sydney · Toronto
Astronaut House, Feltham, Middlesex, England

First published 1967
Second impression 1968
Revised edition 1980
ISBN 0 600 43070 7

Set in 11pt Monophoto Garamond by
Tradespools Limited, Frome

Printed in England by
Hazell, Watson & Viney Limited
Aylesbury

Contents

	INTRODUCTION	7
1	ROMAN BRITAIN	9
2	ANGLO-SAXON AND MEDIEVAL, *c.*500–1500	12
3	TUDOR AND EARLY STUART, *c.*1500–1660	23
4	THE LATER STUARTS, 1660–1714	37
	Charles II, 1660–85	37
	William and Mary, 1689–1702	41
	Queen Anne, 1702–14	48
5	THE GEORGIAN PERIOD, 1714–1830	52
	Early Georgian: the Pre-Chippendale Era, 1714–50	52
	Chippendale and the Rococo, *c.*1750–65	61
	'Country' Chairs	68
	Windsor Chairs	70
	Adam, Hepplewhite and the Neo-Classical, *c.*1765–90	73
	Sheraton, *c.*1790–1800	80
	Regency, *c.*1800–30	82
6	EARLY VICTORIAN, *c.*1830–60	88
7	LATE VICTORIAN AND EDWARDIAN, *c.*1860–1914	99
8	MODERN TRENDS	107
	GLOSSARY OF CHAIRS	114
	INDEX	127
	ACKNOWLEDGMENTS	128

Introduction

THE CHAIR predominates in any study of English furniture. It is one of the earliest recorded pieces. From its beginnings it has been used as a symbol of authority and even now, in these days of mass-production, this meaning has not entirely been lost. As it has passed into the currency of everyday use, into the humblest homes, it has provided an index of improved living standards, and in its diverse forms it has faithfully reflected the many activities (and inactivities) of domestic life, formal and informal – eating and drinking; polite conversation and gossip; study, reading and writing; and recreation, leisure and comfort. No other piece of furniture has been given so many descriptive labels. Some of these are contemporary; many are modern (and often unauthorised); all indicate a mixture of the functional and romantic which the chair's different uses, and its long history, readily explain.

Nor can any other piece serve so usefully as a guide to stylistic changes, for the best chairs have been the first to exhibit the materials and decorative forms dictated by the latest fashion. At the present day, when the study of human comfort approaches the status of a new science, it is still the chair which remains the focal point of interest. At the same time, in some forms it has sturdily maintained its character as a folk piece, an example of the unsophisticated taste of the countryside and of the craftsman's use of local materials for local needs, and it is significant that one of the most popular chairs in production today has retained its traditional shape, with little alteration, for some three centuries.

In many respects the English chair-maker has been greatly indebted to foreign styles and techniques. These, however, have usually been translated into true English versions, and the traffic has not been one-way, for thousands of English chairs have been exported since the 17th century to all parts of the globe; it would need a separate study to trace their considerable influence on

7

foreign chair design. It is noteworthy that English chairs were held in particularly high esteem abroad in Victoria's reign, which is so often excluded from studies of English furniture.

This book attempts to examine as many aspects of the development of English chairs as its length allows, beginning with those of Roman Britain and continuing to those of the Modern Movement. Brief reference is made to other forms of seating furniture.

A Glossary has been added to this new and revised edition, which I hope will be of interest and use to the reader.

My special thanks are due once again to Mr Michael Barnes for his careful line drawings.

The reference to the Duke of Cumberland's furniture at Windsor Great Lodge (1765) is included by gracious permission of Her Majesty the Queen.

Edward T. Joy

CHAPTER ONE

Roman Britain

CLASSICAL FORMS and decoration, which were to play so important a part in the history of English furniture, particularly during their revival in the late Stuart and the Georgian periods, were found in Britain long before the arrival of the Anglo-Saxons, during the four centuries of Roman rule which preceded the Anglo-Saxon settlements of the 5th century A.D. Though Britain was an outlying province of the Roman Empire it shared much of the civilisation inherited by Rome from the older Mediterranean cultures and their forms of art and handicraft.

Chairs and seats of a ceremonial character must have been used in Roman Britain as they were throughout the rest of the Empire. The symbolic grandeur of the throne or chair of state goes right back in history to the Minoan kings' stone throne, reputed to be the oldest in Europe, which survived the destruction of the Palace of Knossos, Crete, *c.* 1400 B.C., and is still in its original position. Equally fascinating are the thrones of the Egyptian Pharaohs, of which the most famous example is probably the one of carved wood, plated with gold and inlaid with semi-precious stones, made *c.* 1350 B.C., which was discovered in Tutankhamen's tomb in 1922. The Egyptians were craftsmen of considerable skill; they developed various forms of thrones, chairs and stools with a mastery of the techniques of veneering, inlay, gilding and jointing of a standard which was not equalled in England until comparatively recent times.

The Greeks brought beauty into the development of the chair with the *klismos*, a graceful version, apparently based on a simpler type of throne, with forward-curving front legs (of 'sabre' form) balanced by the opposing curves of the rear legs, which swept upwards into the back to a curved horizontal backboard for the sitter's shoulders. This type was to become very fashionable in Regency England.

1. Reconstruction of a wickerwork chair of the type used in Roman Britain.
Roman Museum, Bath.

It is likely that the Romano-British ruling classes used the *solium*, or chair of state, and the *sella curulis*, or curule, the magistrates' seat, shaped like a camp stool so that it could be folded up for easy transport on the chariot (or *currus*) from which the stool takes its name. Stools of a special kind were sometimes invested with the same importance as chairs. It is also likely that the *klismos* was known in town houses and country villas, but no direct evidence of its use has been found.

Unfortunately, the perishable nature of most furniture, even when metal was used, has meant that our knowledge of furniture in Roman Britain is limited by fragmentary remains discovered by archaeologists, an additional source of information being the sculptured furniture carved on tombstones and depicted on a variety of statuary.

There are a number of carved stone representations of a chair with continuous back and sides on a rectangular or semicircular base. Some examples were apparently covered with leather or upholstery, but typical examples were of wickerwork. This type, known throughout the western provinces of the Empire, is shown, for instance, on the tomb of Julia Velva, found on the Mount at York and now in the Yorkshire Museum there. What is of particular interest is that the craft of basketry, of which wickerwork is a variety, was known in Britain before the Roman occupation, for examples of this have been found in the Glastonbury lake village (about 100 B.C.). There is little doubt, therefore, that the wickerwork chairs of Roman Britain were made by skilled native craftsmen, and a careful reconstruction of one in the Roman Museum, Bath, against a background of mosaic floor and panelled walls, has special attraction because it was made by local craftsmen who can claim (since Glastonbury is near Bath) to be continuing one of the very oldest of British chair-making crafts (*illus. 1*). The wicker chair may well have been the matron's seat in the Romano-British household.

Another type of chair, seen, for example, on a statue found at Housesteads on the Roman Wall, is straight-backed, and may have had straight legs joined by stretchers. There is also evidence of four-legged stools (some may have been made of metal) and of folding stools, of the curule type, but intended for domestic use, with either straight or curved leg.

CHAPTER TWO

Anglo-Saxon and Medieval

c. 500 — 1500

ALMOST NOTHING is known of the furniture of the Anglo-Saxon period – which extended in time from the collapse of Roman rule in the 5th century A.D. until the Norman Conquest of 1066 – for none has survived and few facts are recorded about it. The furniture skills of the classical world disappeared in Britain after the withdrawal of the Roman legions. From earliest times, however, it is clear that the great hall of the king or tribal chieftain, which was a centre of community life and was used as council chamber, guest house, banqueting room and even sleeping quarters, was the main setting for such furniture as was then made, and that seating arrangements conformed to an accepted social pattern which had been familiar to the English in their continental homeland.

Such facts are revealed in *Beowulf*, the great Anglo-Saxon epic of the 8th century. The exploits of the hero, Beowulf, take place in the 6th century among the Danish and Swedish tribes who were the near neighbours of the Germanic ancestors of the Anglo-Saxons. Much of the scene of the poem is set in the great timbered hall of the Danish king. Here the throne is always reserved for the king. On one occasion it is referred to as the 'treasure throne', the seat of honour from which the king dispenses rewards to his followers. Though the queen is entitled to take her seat beside her husband, all others sit on benches, even the leading men of state when they attend a great banquet in Beowulf's honour. After the feasting, when the king and queen retire to their own apartments, the rest of the company clear the benches away and sleep on the floor of the hall.

Throughout the Anglo-Saxon period, and for most of the succeeding medieval period (which we may take as ending at about 1500), all the furniture, apart from the lord's chair, in halls such as that described in *Beowulf*, was made to be easily moved about, so that it could be set up and cleared away rapidly. Tables were simply loose boards placed on rough trestles. The stool was the commonest form of seat, and in fact was the usual term for any kind of seat for a single person. In large medieval households social life continued to be centred on the great hall. It remained the custom for the lord and his retainers to share their meals and entertainments, the high table of the lord and his family standing on a dais at one end, with chairs reserved for the master and mistress, while the retainers sat on stools or benches in the body of the hall. Later, benches or forms – the two terms are interchangeable – were often fixed against the wall, as also were settles (benches with arms and sometimes also backs and boxes beneath the seats), for medieval meals were taken at one side of the tables. Such fixed furniture was known as 'dormante' in contemporary literature. The stool was thus the most movable type of seat.

The little medieval furniture that there was led a nomadic life. It was literally carted about by its royal or baronial owners when they moved between their palaces, castles, halls and manor houses, superintending their domains, administering justice, keeping order, and getting their food from the manors through which they passed or from the deer forests. There could be no elegance about such furniture; it was intended for rough usage, and no great skill was required for its construction. Chests and coffers, which could store valuables and also be used as seats, tables and beds if necessary, and stools, benches, settles and trestle tables which, as has been seen, were always being shifted about the hall, were all obviously pieces of the greatest practical value, for they could easily be stacked on carts for their periodic travels. The change from movable to 'dormante' furniture towards the end of the Middle Ages is a clear indication of the coming of more settled conditions. The nomadic character of early furniture is still commemorated today in the many European languages – but not English – in which 'furniture' and 'movables' are the same word (*meubles, muebles, mobilia, möbeln, meubelen,* etc.).

Medieval domestic furniture was almost exclusively the possession of the wealthy classes. For the rest of the population, furniture had hardly a place in a life that was rough, unhealthy and insecure, far removed from the romantic picture of the period which William Morris and his contemporaries painted in the 19th century.

2. Oak chair of *c.* 1250; carved with Gothic tracery, it was once probably part of a set of stalls. St Mary's Church, Little Dunmow, Essex.

In trying to establish what kinds of chairs were in use in the early Middle Ages, we are faced with the problem that very few examples have survived, and none earlier than the 13th and 14th centuries. Moreover, as these survivors seem originally to have been made for churches, and formed part of a set of stalls, they have undergone much alteration in the process of survival. Nevertheless, we can assume that these chairs, like other church and monastic pieces, were similar to those in great houses, and this is confirmed by examples in illustrated manuscripts and paintings, the chief sources of our information on the furniture of the period. An oak chair in

3. The Coronation Chair of *c.* 1300, the most famous example of a medieval chair of state. Still splendid, though much diminished from its original splendour, this oak chair once had leopards and turrets on its pinnacles, the whole being richly coloured and partially gilded. Westminster Abbey.

St Mary's Church, Little Dunmow, Essex, probably a relic of a set of stalls and now much changed, is considered to have been made *c.*1250. It is carved with simple Gothic tracery on the back and sides (*illus.* 2).

A famous oak chair in St Mary's Guildhall, Coventry, dates from *c.*1450. It is the remnant of a triple seat made for the Masters of the three united guilds of St Mary, St John the Baptist and St Catherine, for whom the Hall was built, and this single survivor has a carved representation of the Virgin and Child on one side. The rest of this side, the part below the seat, and both surfaces

4. Originally part of a triple throne, this chair of oak dates from the mid 15th century. It is carved with vine scrolls and Perpendicular Gothic tracery; the royal lions of England and the arms of Coventry form the finials. St Mary's Guildhall, Coventry.

of the back, are carved with Perpendicular Gothic tracery: the lower part of the other side is left plain. Richly carved vine leaves and tendrils decorate the flat edges of the sloping arms, and continue down the front. There are two finials, one the royal lions of England, the other the arms of Coventry (the elephant and castle) (*illus*. 4). Drawings of it appear in two early 19th-century books inspired by the revived interest in medieval furniture – Henry Shaw's *Specimens of Ancient Furniture* (1836) and Richard Bridgens's *Furniture with Candelabra and Interior Decoration* (1838). Shaw points out that the mortises (*illus*. 7) on the side of the chair with the plain lower part indicate that it was one of a set, and in fact these features prove that it was the right-hand seat (that of St Mary's Guild) of the original triple throne. A portrait of Richard II (1377–99) in Westminster Abbey shows him seated on a similar chair, with the same kind of carved decoration.

The throne-like chair, known as a chair of state (or estate) figures prominently in medieval records. It was obviously intended for persons of the highest rank and is often shown as a magnificent towering structure surmounted by a canopy of wainscot or of rich material. It stood on a dais against the wall with a 'dosser' (or dorcer) of tapestry, embroidery or other rich fabric on the back, and a 'banker', a cushion or covering, on the seat. Most of these chairs must have been much too bulky to have followed their owners on their travels, and were left behind in the empty hall, stripped of their coverings. Some, however, were moved about, for the Ewelme Inventory of 1466 mentions that the Duke of Suffolk's 'chaire of tymbre of astate' had 'a case of lether thereto' into which it was packed for removal.

The most famous example of the medieval chair of state is the Coronation Chair in Westminster Abbey. Made *c*. 1300 of oak – though apparently originally designed to be made in metal – it is an architectural composition, with a decorated pedimented gable and two pinnacles at the back, and carved Gothic tracery at the sides. The Stone of Scone, Edward I's trophy from his Scottish wars, lies below the seat in a platform which is open at the front and has two pierced quatrefoils at the sides. In its present condition the chair gives us only the faintest idea of its original magnificence. The leopards and turrets which should be standing on its pinnacles were removed early in the 19th century; four lions have been

5. Oak X-frame chair of *c.* 1550, originally covered with blue velvet.
Bishop Gardner's Chapel, Winchester Cathedral.

added at some time to the base; and the woodwork has been mutilated (*illus. 3*). Above all, the chair should be richly coloured, with gilding predominant. Not only is this indicated by evidence that the 'king's painter' was responsible for the decoration, but all available information also shows that medieval woodwork of this kind, if it were not covered with costly materials, was brightly painted or gilded. This is also true of medieval cathedral choir stalls, whose present plain deep brown colour, attractive though it is, is quite different in its decorative appearance from what the original designers intended.

Other types of chairs were made for people less exalted than those entitled to sit in elaborate chairs of state. The traditional X-frame chair was more convenient for transporting, and some examples, like the Roman curule, were made to fold up. Such chairs had two X-frames each, either at the sides, braced by stretchers, or at the back and front. Towards the end of the medieval period this type was made by coffer-makers who originally, as their name shows, made the trussing coffers (or 'standards') in which the wealthy stowed their stuffs, plate and other valuables during their progresses. Gradually the coffer-makers came to make other pieces of furniture, principally because they covered such pieces, as they did their coffers, with leather or sometimes velvet and other fabrics. They were not in fact craftsmen in wood, for their skill lay in covering the framework of furniture, but they were the first furniture-makers to achieve the status of royal craftsmen and were found working at court until late Georgian times, still making chests and trunks for storage and transport.

A late medieval X-frame chair from the vestry of York Minster (*Frontispiece*) is illustrated in Shaw's *Specimens* and there is a famous post-medieval example in Winchester Cathedral (now in Bishop Gardner's Chapel) which by tradition was used at Queen Mary's wedding to Philip II of Spain in the Cathedral on 25 July 1554. Made of oak, it was originally covered with blue velvet fastened with gilt nails. It is one of the few surviving examples of the coffer-maker's craft (*illus. 5*).

The wooden framework of many of these earlier medieval chairs was not nearly so important, even in the largest examples, as the decoration or upholstery. The woodwork fell largely within the province of the carpenters, who employed quite primitive techniques to produce the framework for their much more skilled colleagues, the carvers, gilders, coffer-makers and upholders (the name, until quite recent times, for upholsterers), to complete. There was, however, another traditional type of chair – the turned or 'thrown' variety – which was produced by the turners on their lathes. Forms of knob- or ball-turning appear on a faldstool (literally a folding stool, but one, in this instance, invested with ceremonial significance) and on an elbow chair illustrated in the Eadwine Psalter, which was written by Eadwine, a monk at Canterbury, *c*.1150, and is now in the library of Trinity College, Cambridge. A ladder-back type of chair, with 'rungs' of turned spindles, was also in use, but a common type, which there is some evidence for believing was of Scandinavian origin and which was introduced into England by the Normans (who gave the word 'chair' to the English language), had a triangular seat into which three sturdy turned posts were fixed at the corners. A plain variety, as it developed towards the end of the medieval period, had bobbin-turned arms linking the front posts to a horizontal board for supporting the shoulders on the back post, while turned stretchers connected the bottom of the three posts just above floor level. A more elaborate version had a back framework built up of a variety of ornamental spindles, and connected to the front posts by ringed rails; a series of spindles joined the front stretcher to the seat. This type, becoming more and more ornate, was made until well into the Stuart period, in a variety of patterns.

In August 1761, Horace Walpole refers to these medieval chairs in a letter to George Montagu from Strawberry Hill, when he records that a friend 'has picked up a whole cloister full of old chairs in Herefordshire. He bought them one by one, here and there in farm-houses, for three-and-sixpence and a crown apiece. They are of wood, the seats triangular, the backs, arms and legs loaded with turnery.' Walpole requests that some may be bought for him in Cheshire, adding: 'Take notice, no two need be of the same pattern.' But though considerable numbers of these chairs must have been made throughout the medieval period, surviving examples date only from the 17th century (*illus. 6*).

Like basketry, turning has an ancient connection with chair-making which has continued into modern times. The turned ladder-back chair was elevated into a fashionable piece, with suitable refinements, in the Chippendale period, and was revived in its simple traditional form by Ernest Gimson in the 1890s. It was the turners who ultimately produced the Windsor chair which has retained its basic character for more than three centuries. English turned chair styles have spread their influence far beyond their rural workshops, for they were taken overseas to the American colonies in the 17th century and given a fresh lease of life in the homesteads of the early settlers.

During the 14th century slowly improving standards of living and changes in domestic life began to encourage the production of better and more varied furniture. Internal and external trade was stimulated by markets and fairs, in which English woollen cloth, the best in Europe, played a leading part. A prosperous merchant class emerged. Towns, gaining freedom and power through the purchase of charters from the crown and aristocracy, fostered craft guilds who enforced high standards of craftsmanship with increasing specialisation. As feudalism decayed and the old aristocracy was killed off in the Wars of the Roses (1455–85), furniture gradually lost its nomadic character, though it was still far from achieving comfort. The interior of the large house was changing; by the 15th century some houses had a great chamber and a dining-parlour in which the family could take their meals in private.

During this later period the joiners made their own particular contribution to chair-making, and thus added to the list of craftsmen already concerned with the making, decorating and finishing of chairs – the carpenters, basketmakers and turners, the painters, gilders and carvers, and the coffer-makers and upholders. The joiners employed the constructional technique of the panel and frame. The framework of vertical stiles and horizontal rails was secured by mortise and tenon joints, the mortise being the socket in the stile into which the tenon, the corresponding projection on the rail, fitted exactly. The panel, tapered on all sides, fitted into grooves on the inside of the frame and was allowed sufficient movement to prevent warping. 'Joinery' thus meant greater strength and greater economy of material (*illus. 7, 9*).

The result was the box-like joined or panel-back chair, probably derived from the chest, with panelled back, sides and seat, without legs, and with arms provided by the flat rails of the side panels.

This type continued to be made until the end of the 16th century. At first the panels were decorated with carved Gothic tracery and the linen-fold pattern, which was most probably of 15th-century Flemish origin and takes its name from its supposed resemblance to folded linen. There was a close connection between England and Flanders at this time and much Flemish furniture was imported into England, including chairs of 'Flaunders worke' which are listed in inventories, but which have not so far been identified.

The joiner was destined to play an important part in the development of the chair. Until the end of the Georgian period chair-making was always regarded as specialist joinery work and as 'a branch', so Sheraton writes in his *Cabinet Dictionary* (1803), 'generally confined to itself; as those who professedly work at it seldom engage to make cabinet furniture'. Long after the original type of joined chair had become obsolete, the skilled joiner kept alive the tradition of the chair of state by making thrones and ceremonial seats for the court (where the royal joiner was styled 'Joiner and Chair-Maker' and was entitled to wear livery as a symbol of his ancient office) and for ambassadors, the Inns of Court, Livery Companies and the like.

The stool also changed its form in the late 15th century. Earlier stools had circular tops into which three splayed legs were socketed. Some also had triangular seats. These tripods were insecure seats – to fall between two stools must have been a common occurrence – and the improved kinds had solid, sloped, trestle ends tenoned through the rectangular seat and slotted to receive two apron pieces for greater stability.

The traditional authority and distinction of the chair are quite clearly evident today, in spite of the vastly changed conditions of our times. Its symbolism is retained in the deference paid to the chairman of a meeting, and in particular to the Speaker of the House of Commons, who occupies the only chair while all other members, even cabinet ministers, sit on benches; in the mythical 'chairs' of University professors; and in the chairing of prize-winners. A cathedral is so named because, as the principal church in a bishop's diocese, it contains his throne (or *cathedra*).

CHAPTER THREE

Tudor and Early Stuart

c. 1500–1660

THE REFORMATION affected the development of English furniture in the Tudor period in two main ways: it broke the direct link with the Italian Renaissance and it helped to create a new class of wealthy landowners who became the patrons of English craftsmen in Elizabeth I's reign (1558–1603).

In the earlier part of his reign Henry VIII (1509–47) had encouraged Italian artists and craftsmen to work in England, and as a result a limited application of classical Renaissance decoration was introduced into English houses. But when Henry finally rejected papal authority by his Act of Supremacy of 1534, these fruitful contacts largely ceased. England's closest cultural ties were now with the Protestants of the Low Countries, and it was their flamboyant interpretation of the Renaissance, widely disseminated by their printed pattern books of engraved designs of architecture and furniture, which exercised the strongest influence on English design and decoration after 1550. Further stimulus came from 1566 onwards with the influx of Flemish craftsmen fleeing to England from the Duke of Alva's persecution of the Protestants in the Netherlands. Not until the next century did the Italian version of the Renaissance reach England.

The dissolution of the monasteries in 1536 and 1539 and the sale of their estates by the crown saw the emergence of a landed class eager to exploit the possibilities of agriculture, industry and trade. Many of these newly rich built large houses which were quite different in appearance and internal arrangement from previous ones. The Reformation also shifted the emphasis entirely from ecclesiastical to domestic architecture, and new standards of comfort and furnishing were achieved. The house lost its defensive character; the moat was replaced by a garden, and inside, in addition to the great chamber, dining-parlour and private rooms, there was now the long gallery, an Elizabethan innovation, which stretched the whole length of the upper story and was used for family gatherings and entertainments, and for exercise during the winter months.

One of the problems in the study of early Tudor furniture is the difficulty of resolving how much of it was imported from abroad, how much was made by foreign craftsmen working in England, and how much was produced by English craftsmen. Since the beginning of the 16th century foreign craftsmen working in England had aroused the envy of English workers, and the notorious riots of 'Evil May Day', 1517, when London apprentices rose against aliens, were due, according to Hall's *Chronicle*, to the fact that 'poor English Artificers could scarce get any living'. Dutchmen, it was said, were bringing over 'wainscot already wrought, as . . . cupboards, stools, tables, chests. . .'

Some magnificent upholstered and painted chairs, obviously for ceremonial use, appear in the inventories of furniture of royal

6. Oak turned ('thrown') chair of 17th-century date, of the type made in England since medieval times.

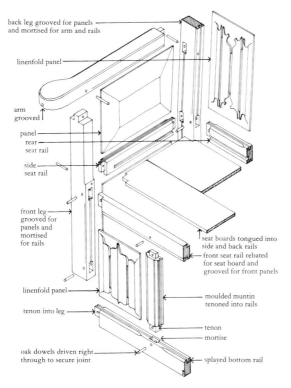

back leg grooved for panels
and mortised for arm and rails

linenfold panel

arm
grooved

panel
rear
seat rail

side
seat rail

front leg
grooved for
panels and
mortised
for rails

seat boards tongued into
side and back rails

front seat rail rebated
for seat board and
grooved for front panels

linenfold panel

moulded muntin
tenoned into rails

tenon into leg

tenon

mortise

oak dowels driven right
through to secure joint

splayed bottom rail

7. Construction of panel-back chair.

palaces and a few great houses of the early Tudor period, such as those of Cardinal Wolsey, the Vyne, Hampshire (1541), and Henry VIII (1547). No doubt some of these were made abroad or copied from foreign examples. Their description does not enable us to identify them, and none seem to have survived, but it is likely that a number were of the traditional X-shape which returned to fashion in the Tudor period, and this type was certainly made by English coffer-makers, particularly by members of the Green family – successively William, John and Thomas – who were royal coffer-makers from *c.* 1530 until the end of the century. Like the example in Winchester Cathedral, these chairs had their framework completely covered with rich materials, and had seats of loose squab cushions resting on 'girthweb' or webbing.

Richly upholstered chairs continued to be made throughout the 16th century. When Lord John Lumley died, the 'true inventory of all such movables as were found in Lumley Castle' (1609) included the following among a large number of other chairs and stools:

3 chaires of cloth of gold and silver wth a long quishion [cushion]
  of the same. . . . . xv^{li} [£15]
One purple cloth of gold chayre wth a long quishion price . . . iii^{li}
Two needle work chaires wth two long quishions of the same price iii^{li}
Two chaires one of crimson silk and gold the other of crimson silk
  and silver wth two little stooles price . . . . iii^{li}
Two purple velvett chaires and iii purple velvett quishions and a
  little stoole price . . . . v^{li}

Stools were made *en suite* with such chairs, for use both as ordinary seats and as footstools. After 1550 the joined (or joint) stool came into use. This had four turned legs, straddling outwards, joined to a rail beneath the seat and linked just above floor level by stretchers (*illus.* 8). A favourite upholstery material of the time for chairs and stools was 'Turkey work', so named, not because it resembled the design on Turkey carpets, but because, like them, it was woven

8. Oak panel-back armchair and stool, with carved and fluted supports;
latter part of the 16th century.

9. Panel-back ('joyned') chair of *c.* 1525–50; the oak is carved with linen-fold decoration and, on the top panel, Renaissance ornament. Victoria and Albert Museum, London.

10. Oak armchair of *c.* 1600; of *caquetoire* type, it has shaped rails at the base and supports beneath the centre of the arms.

11. Back view of above; the rear stretcher is missing.

with a knotted woollen pile (it is thus also often described as 'Turkey worked' or 'work't').

The joined or panel-back chair underwent significant changes in this period. A distinctly light type, known as the *caquetoire* from its supposed use as a conversation chair (French, *caqueter*, to chatter or gossip) appeared before 1550. It varied considerably in design, but was generally distinguished by a tall, narrow, rectangular back often decorated with carving, and was open beneath the arms and seat (*illus. 10, 11*). Much more freedom of treatment of the arms and front legs became possible when the panels beneath the seat and arms were discarded, as can be seen when this occurred on the traditional panel-back. As long as these panels were retained, the arms, arm supports and legs, which were components of the frame, were straight and square. With the panels gone, the arms could be curved to support the elbow, and scrolled beyond the supports, while both arm supports and front legs could be turned (*illus. 8*).

Many Elizabethan panel-back chairs were decorated with inlay and strapwork, two features which came to England from the Low Countries. Inlay (then called 'markatre') was formed by setting small sections of woods of different colours about $\frac{1}{8}$ inch below the surface of the decorated area. Floral and chequered patterns were favoured, the former being often found on the backs of finer chairs (*illus. 13*). The chief woods used for inlaying were bog oak, box, holly, sycamore and pear. Strapwork was a continuous decoration of flat, interlaced geometrical patterns carved in low relief (*illus. 12*). A great many crude versions of conventional classical designs were also carved on chairs, such as a round arch on the back, and guilloches on the 'head' and 'ear' pieces superimposed at the top and sides. The decoration generally reflected the flamboyant character of the Elizabethan age, but the turned arm supports and front legs were often of graceful appearance, in marked contrast to the grotesque 'bulbs' on tables and court cupboards.

Two distinctive types of chair, introduced after 1550, further demonstrated the tendency towards lightness and portability. One was the back stool, the first chair without arms; the other was the folding chair.

The back stool seems to have developed from the change which

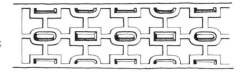

12. Strapwork decoration; end of 16th century.

13. Oak enclosed chair with panelled back and inlaid floral decoration; early 17th century.

14. 'Farthingale chair' or 'back stool' of *c*. 1625, one of a set of six. Made of beech, with turned columnar front legs, the uprights and stretchers are, unusually, decorated with painted flowers and leaves. Knole Park, Kent.

15. Detail of upholstered X-frame chair of *c.* 1610 showing the contemporary appliqué of cloth of gold on crimson satin. Knole Park, Kent.

occurred in seating arrangements when the separate dining-parlour for the family became usual in large households. As the table now stood in the centre of the room and no longer on the raised dais at the end of the hall, the master and mistress occupied chairs at each end of the table while the rest of the family and guests sat on stools at the sides, the difference in seats observing the time-honoured differences in status. Those sitting on stools lacked the support for their backs which the wall had formerly provided for them, and so the back legs of the stools were continued upwards into uprights which were linked by one or two rails or a panel, and were tilted slightly backwards. The conventions were not violated for these single chairs (as they are now called) were regarded as stools. The term 'back stool' was still in use in the latter half of the 18th century; it can be found, for instance, in Ince and Mayhew's pattern book, *The Universal System of Household Furniture* (1759–62), in the bill for chairs made by Katherine Naish, the royal joiner, for St James's Palace in 1759, and in Francis Hervé's bill of 1791 (charging £14. 5s. for six back stools) to Lady Spencer at Althorp, Northants. But already in the 17th century the terms 'elbow chairs' and 'back chairs' were also being used to distinguish chairs with arms from those without (*illus. 14*).

The folding chair was an improved lighter version which closely resembled Italian models. The arms, which were shaped to support the elbows, were hinged by a wooden rod passing through the top of the front legs and the sides of the seat. Carved round arches enclosing a lozenge were a typical decoration of the back. These have sometimes been called 'Glastonbury' chairs after an example in Shaw's *Specimens* (1836), in which it is described as 'the Abbot's chair, Glastonbury' and incorrectly dated to Henry VIII's reign (*illus. 17*).

To all these kinds of chair of the 16th century can be added the wicker and turned chairs, traditional since medieval times.

In the early 17th century increasing numbers of richly up-holstered chairs were made for large houses. One well-known surviving example of this period which is now, with its footstool, in the Victoria and Albert Museum formerly belonged to William Juxon, Archbishop of Canterbury. It is of X-shape, upholstered in crimson velvet, trimmed with galon (a decorative braid) and studded with brass-headed nails. Tradition says that it was used by Charles I at his trial in Westminster Hall. Its frame is of beech, a wood particularly liable to attack by worm, which explains why surviving chairs of this kind are so rare. There are, however, some fine examples at Knole Park, Kent, which date from James I's reign (1603–25) (*illus. 15*).

High-class chair-making was the work of the joiner, who saw to the framework, and of the upholsterer, who covered it. These functions were carefully divided, as the Lord Chamberlain's

16. 'Yorkshire and Derbyshire' chair of *c.* 1660 with hooped carved rails centring in a head with a pointed beard. Victoria and Albert Museum, London.

records, detailing the work of royal craftsmen, clearly show. Nicholas Reade, for instance, the court joiner to the first two Stuarts, prepared (and repaired) the timber work of chairs and stools of all kinds – chairs of state, 'folding chayres', 'carrieing chayres' (with iron handles), 'X chaires', and 'back chaires', and high stools, footstools and 'walnuttree joyned stooles'. Nowhere is he concerned with upholstery. On the other hand, his contemporary, Ralph Grinder, the court upholsterer, concentrated on

17. Folding chair ('Glastonbury' type) of *c.* 1600; the arches are carved with guilloches and lozenges. Victoria and Albert Museum, London.

18. Chair-table dated 1627. The Great Hall, Cotehele House, Cornwall (*see* p. 116).

the coverings. In 1623, for example, he was paid £2. 3s. 4d. for 'covering two chaires of state of crimson gould tissue, and for fustian, downe, girthwebb and buckram, guilt nailes and bullion nailes', together with tasselled cushions and baize cases. Reade's bills show, incidentally, how many different types of chairs and stools were in fashionable use *c.* 1625.

A broader version of the back stool with upholstered seat and back which was made at this time is now popularly known as a 'farthingale chair'. Though this description seems to have originated, like so many others, in Victorian times and was not contemporary, it nevertheless seems reasonable to suppose that these wide, armless seats were intended for the convenience of women wearing the extravagantly hooped farthingale dress (*illus. 14, 24*).

The middle years of the 17th century, from the Civil War until the end of the Commonwealth in 1660, saw the triumph of Puritanism. Austerity checked the production of lavishly upholstered chairs. In contrast, however, to the plain decoration which was usual at the time, back stools, which were developing more and more in the direction of what are now designated single chairs, often made free use of bobbin, ball and ring turning on legs and stretchers. The split baluster, a form of decoration dating back to Elizabeth's reign, was also frequently found; a turned baluster was split vertically and the two matching halves were glued to the uprights of the chair.

A plain type of back stool of *c.* 1650 had its seat and back covered with leather tacked on with rows of brass nails. Another variety, now known as the 'Yorkshire and Derbyshire' chair owing to its association with those two areas (and also with Lancashire), was made in the late 1650s until after the Restoration. This latter type employed two main methods of filling the back – either with two wide, flat hoops decorated with carving and attached pendants, or with an open arcade of turned balusters between two connecting rails. A carved head with a pointed beard which can sometimes be found in the centre of the arched tops has been said to commemorate Charles I and to reflect the royalist sympathies of northern England after his execution. Though this may be possible, there seems to be no contemporary authority for the name 'mortuary' chair which has been given to this particular type (*illus. 16*).

CHAPTER FOUR

The Later Stuarts
1660–1714

CHARLES II, 1660–85

The year 1660, when Charles II was restored to the throne, can make a very good claim to be considered the most important single date in the history of English furniture, for it opened England to the full impact of foreign styles and technical processes. Charles and his luxury-loving court were determined to enjoy in England the comfort and elegance to which they had become accustomed during their eleven-year exile. In the words of John Evelyn, the diarist, written at the time of Charles's death, the king 'brought in a politer way of living which passed to luxury and intolerable expense'. Landowners and merchants, growing increasingly prosperous and throwing off the austerity of Puritan rule, eagerly followed the court's example. The Great Fire of London in 1666 unexpectedly hastened progress, for the neater and more comfortable houses of brick and stone, no longer of timber, that were now built in the city and expanding suburbs, required a vast amount of light and compact furniture, far different from the bulky pieces of the previous period.

The new styles, techniques and types of furniture were mainly introduced by immigrant foreign craftsmen working in London for the wealthier classes. But their skills were so rapidly absorbed by English craftsmen that within a generation well-made furniture of an unmistakable English character, beginning to match the best continental standards, made its appearance. By 1700 English furniture was being exported throughout Europe, where it was widely admired (*illus. 19*).

The new fashions ended the long reign of oak as far as the finest pieces were concerned. For the rich, the new wood was walnut, which was carved, turned or applied as a veneer to show off its beautiful figure. The technique of marquetry led to the emergence of the English cabinet-maker.

37

19. Furniture exports from London to Spain in 1700 included chairs to the value of £642. 7s.

Chair design was to vary considerably between 1660 and 1700, but, strangely enough, the first new type to appear after the Restoration was a simple, light and cheap cane chair, already familiar in Holland and France, which was specifically designed for comfort and which, contrary to the usual development, was in use in ordinary homes before being taken up by fashionable makers. The cane-work found on the panelled backs and seats of chairs and other seating furniture was a large and coarse mesh of split rattans which came from a kind of palm grown in the Far East and which were imported by the East India Company. The early cane chairs had flat arms curved along their length, and backs slightly hollowed for the sitter's comfort.

The main decoration was provided by spiral turning of the uprights, legs and stretchers, which were mortised and tenoned into rectangular blocks where they joined each other. Such chairs were said to be 'turned all over'. A shallow herring-bone stamping often decorated the back frame and the top and side edges of the seat rail. The inexpensive mechanical methods of turning and

20. Upholstered walnut armchair with spiral arms and framework, *c.* 1665.
Victoria and Albert Museum, London.

stamping cut down the costs of production, and many of these chairs, which were usually made in sets of two armchairs and six or more single chairs, must have been found in houses, particularly those rebuilt in London after 1666, which formerly had only stools.

The design of these cane chairs was admirable, but much of their simplicity and good proportions were lost when, about the middle of Charles's reign, they became part of the furniture of great houses. Their backs became increasingly higher and their decoration more elaborate. A deeper cresting was adopted and a broad, flat stretcher replaced the turned rail connecting the front legs. Both the cresting and flat stretcher were lavishly carved, at first on a solid ground and later with pierced work, in matching decoration often in the form of a crown supported by amorini, or of flowers, foliage and eagles' heads. The arms, now of round or oval section, curved downwards in the centre and scrolled over the supports. Elongated scrolls were also used for arm supports and front legs. With spiral turning on the uprights and back and side stretchers, these elaborate chairs fully expressed the flamboyancy of the reign. The best chairs were of walnut, but beech, stained to resemble walnut, was used for less expensive kinds (*illus.* 21).

The popularity of cane chairs of all types alarmed upholsterers and woollen manufacturers, who unsuccessfully petitioned Parliament to suppress this threat to their livelihood. Writing in 1690 Nicholas Barbon (*A Discourse of Trade*) describes cane chairs as 'being grown too cheap and common', and this date may well have marked the height of their popularity, but they continued to be made until well into the 18th century. According to Daniel Defoe (*The Complete English Tradesman*, 1726) their manufacture was centred in London. In the 1740s their fashion had declined so much that cane chair-makers were also making other varieties, as is noted by an anonymous writer in 1747 (*A General Description of All Trades*): '. . . the Cane-chair-makers not only make this Sort (now almost out of Use) but the better Sort of matted, Leatherbottomed and Wooden Chairs'. Cane-seated chairs, however, never went entirely out of production and became very popular again in the last quarter of the 18th century.

The more elaborate cane chairs of Charles II's reign were obviously inspired by continental models, but English independence clearly asserted itself. Dutch chairs, for example, had thicker spiral turning, narrower crestings and front stretchers, oval panels in the backs, heavier and bolder arms, and crisper and more intricate carving than their English counterparts, which also, unlike foreign chairs of the same character, had a stretcher between the back legs.

WILLIAM AND MARY, 1689–1702

By about 1689, when William and Mary accepted the English throne after the expulsion of James II, Charles's brother and successor, cane chairs had already begun to shed some of their extravagant ornament. Growing sobriety of design was encouraged by the new tone set at court by 'Dutch William', whom Evelyn describes in 1689 as 'very stately, serious and reserved'. More Dutch cabinet-makers came to England and their furniture

21. Walnut armchair of *c.* 1680, the cresting and stretcher carved with a crown bust supported by amorini. Victoria and Albert Museum, London.
22. Walnut armchair with hooped front stretcher and matching cresting, *c.* 1690.

41

23. Pair of late 17th-century upholstered armchairs with crossed stretchers and original upholstery.

was to have wide influence. Vertical lines, however, remained strongly in favour, and some of the tallest chairs ever seen in England, with backs up to two-and-a-half times the height of the seats, were made in the last decade of the century.

At the beginning of the new reign these chairs were made in a variety of types, but spiral turned uprights were gradually replaced by balusters which were turned in graceful forms. Scrolled front legs were still found (*illus*. 22), but *c*. 1690 straight front legs, either baluster turned or square and tapering, with a square-, pear-, or mushroom-shaped capping, became more common. To

24. Japanned 'back stool' with cane seat, of *c.* 1675, one of a set at Ham House in Surrey, a 17th-century house with a superb collection of Charles II furnishings. A coronet and the cypher, 'E.D.', of Elizabeth Dysart, who later became the duchess, appear on the cresting. The backs of these chairs are also painted, suggesting that they were intended for informal groupings away from the wall, unusual for the time, perhaps for taking tea.

increase the height of the backs the arched cresting was fixed above the uprights instead of being tenoned between them. Both cresting and front stretcher were decorated with bold matching scrolls (*illus. 21*). The backs were filled either with cane, which was now of very fine mesh, or, in some examples, with scrollwork and pierced foliage. Some chairs dispensed with the front stretcher altogether and instead had curved X-shaped stretchers which met under the seat in a central finial (*illus. 27, 30*). The very tall and narrow backs had a most graceful appearance, but their pronounced backward rake and the use of dowel jointing instead of mortise and tenon resulted in some structural weakness.

Cane-work never supplanted the rich materials which were used in great variety on the costly upholstered chairs made after 1660. Damask, figured Genoa velvet, embroidered silk, fine needlework, brocatelle, brocade and braid trimmings threaded with gold and silver were all employed, often in brilliant colours. Tasselled fringes, elaborately festooned, were a particular feature of this time.

One of the first orders carried out for Charles II in 1660, immediately after the Restoration, by John Casbert, the court upholsterer, was for 'a crimson velvet french Chayre and five folding stooles, covered all over with gold and silver fringe . . . and Cases of crimson bayes . . . £9. 3s. 6d.' Coverings of baize (as here) and of other materials were used to protect the expensive upholstery. As 'French chayre' was the name for high-backed chairs which originated in France, this extract from the Lord Chamberlain's accounts records one of the first examples made in England. But in general the earliest upholstered chairs which were introduced after 1660 had low backs, like cane chairs and sometimes padded arms, with turned walnut frames (*illus. 20*). Large winged armchairs, described as 'easie' chairs, became fashionable about the middle of Charles's reign. Their framework was polished walnut (*illus. 25*), or beech which was either painted, with gilt ornaments, or gilded all over.

Fine examples of these magnificent chairs are still to be seen at Ham House, Surrey, and Knole, Kent. Those at Ham House are described in two inventories made in 1679 and 1683, and they include two famous 'sleeping chayres, carv'd and guilt frames, covered with crimson and gould stuff with gould fringes'. These are winged chairs with gilded ratchets to adjust the back (*illus. 26*).

The winged armchair won a permanent place in the English home. In William III's reign it often had padded scrolled arms, the legs and stretchers conforming to the changes in design already noted on cane chairs. An elegant type of upholstered chair of the last decade of the century was made without arms. It had a tall, narrow rectangular back which was sometimes shaped at the top.

Many chairs of the late Stuart period were japanned in imitation of oriental lacquered furniture imported by the East India Company. The vogue for this form of decoration spread rapidly after the publication in 1688 of *A Treatise of Japanning and Varnishing* by John Stalker and George Parker. This was a popular illustrated manual which encouraged much amateur effort as well as increased production by professional japanners. The bright colours employed, such as red, green, blue and yellow, often worked as Chinese motifs against a darker background, obviously appealed to the age. But English japan was a poor substitute for genuine lacquer, and few late Stuart japanned chairs have survived.

25. Walnut winged armchair of *c.*1685, with scrolled front legs and stretcher, upholstered in contemporary tapestry.

26. Magnificent 'sleeping chayre', one of a pair, *ensuite* with the
wall-hangings. The carved and gilded frame is richly upholstered in the
original crimson and gold silk. Note front feet, which are sea-horses. The
slope of the back can be adjusted with ratchets, also gilded. Queen's Closet,
Ham House, Surrey.

27. Walnut stool of *c*. 1690, with pear-headed legs and X-form stretchers meeting in a finial; contemporary yellow damask upholstery.

Other forms of seating furniture of the time were made to match a set of chairs and thus followed the same pattern of development in construction, decoration and upholstery. Though the number of chairs had increased, stools were probably the customary form of seat for most people (*illus*. 27). Certainly at court and in large houses they were still used on special occasions by all except distinguished personages and honoured guests for whom the chairs were reserved. Stools varied in shape – square, rectangular and circular – and were sometimes long, with six or eight feet, to accommodate two people. Low footstools were also made. Day beds or couches, already familiar in Shakespeare's day, became very popular after 1660. At first they had cane-work on the seats and raked backs, and were supplemented with mattress and cushions. Later they were fully upholstered. Settees, which developed as the combination of two or three chairs, were established by the end of Queen Anne's reign. Similar in style to settees were 'love seats', a modern name for wide chairs for two people which were introduced early in the 18th century (*illus*. 28).

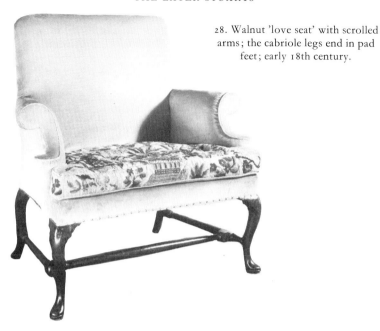

28. Walnut 'love seat' with scrolled arms; the cabriole legs end in pad feet; early 18th century.

QUEEN ANNE, 1702–14

Towards the end of the Stuart period appeared one of the outstanding masterpieces of the English chair-maker's craft, the type now universally known as the 'Queen Anne' chair. The source of inspiration was a new and distinctive type of walnut chair 'in the style of Daniel Marot' which was introduced from Holland about 1700. Marot (1663–1752) was a French Huguenot who had sought religious freedom in Holland and entered the service of William III as architect and designer of interiors and furniture. He visited England where his engraved designs, including furniture, had widespread influence. Already in the 1690s some tall-backed English chairs, decorated with foliage and scrollwork, showed evidence of this. The new chair had a back of curvilinear outline enclosing a central splat which was pierced and carved with foliated ornament. The front legs were of cabriole form united by stretchers. Richard Roberts, appointed joiner to George I in 1715, made a set of this type for Hampton Court Palace (where some still remain) in 1717.

As adapted and transformed in England, the uprights at first

29. (*Left*) Carved and veneered walnut chair of *c*. 1715, the cabriole legs 'hipped' at the seat rail and ending in claw-and-ball feet.
(*Right*) Carved and turned oak chair of *c*. 1700, upholstered with red velvet.
(*Both*) Victoria and Albert Museum, London.

were only slightly curved, but they gradually acquired a more pronounced hoop form relieved by a small angle at the hips. The central splat, which was attached by a moulded 'shoe' to the back rail of the seat, was now solid. It was 'bended' (i.e. curved) at shoulder level for the occupant's comfort, and shaped into varied vase or fiddle forms (*illus. 29 Left*). There is some indication that the central vertical splat of these 'bended-back' chairs may have been inspired by a similar member found on a simple type of Chinese chair with a yoke-shaped top rail which probably reached England via the East India Company.

The name 'cabriole' for the curved chair leg is of Victorian origin (and was in fact a late Georgian term for an armchair with a stuffed back). It was originally applied in France to a leap or bound in dancing, presumably derived from the Italian *capriola*, a goat's leap. In its earliest version on the Continent, the cabriole leg took the form of an animal's leg ending in a hoof foot. English chairs at first used narrow cabrioles with hoof or club feet united by stretchers (*illus. 25*). Gradually the knee pieces became wider and, *c*. 1710, the claw-and-ball foot, a motif probably borrowed from the oriental device of a dragon's claw grasping a pearl, came

30. Pair of side chairs of *c.* 1680, of carved and gilded beech, with unusual crossed stretchers, and retaining their original velvet upholstery.

into use. The plainer club foot however, was found on many chairs until *c.* 1750.

This sturdy leg meant that for the first time stretchers were no longer necessary on English chairs. The chair-maker, working with great skill by hand and eye, through mastery of his material had found that the thrust caused by the sitter's weight is first absorbed inside the leg by the wide knee of the cabriole and then

31. Walnut winged armchair of c. 1710 with cabriole legs and stretchers.

transmitted to the inward curve above the foot, and finally into the foot itself. A straight leg could not absorb the thrust in this way and so required a stretcher to hold it firm. Towards the end of Queen Anne's reign a form known as the 'broken' cabriole, which had a straight four-sided section between knee and foot, was used on a few chairs.

The decoration of curvilinear chairs was carried out with consummate skill. The best examples had carved ornament of acanthus and, later, shells, on the knees, top rail, the centre of the front seat rail, and occasionally on the sides of the splat. Some chairs had their seat rails (which were often rounded at the corners) and their splats veneered with figured burr walnut. This decoration was even applied in some cases to the uprights, which were given a flat surface to take strips of veneer (*illus. 29 Left, 32*). A few outstanding examples were decorated with marquetry, and other exceptional chairs had all four legs of cabriole form, not, as was usual, only the front pair. Many chairs were japanned and others were made in the East from English models, lacquered there, and then exported to England.

CHAPTER FIVE

The Georgian Period
1714–1830

THE GEORGIAN period is universally recognized as the 'golden age' of English furniture. There were cultured wealthy patrons, reared in the classical tradition and with an expert knowledge of European arts and crafts gained at first hand through the grand tour; fine craftsmen who were also very competent designers; architects excelling in achieving a harmony between furniture and carefully planned schemes of interior decoration; and choice woods brought from many parts of the globe – at no other time have inherent good taste and the requisites for high quality of production been so closely knit together.

Among all the fine pieces of the period, English chairs stand out for their gracefulness. They were extensively copied in America and many European countries. Already in the early 18th century some Swedish craftsmen called themselves 'English chair-makers'. In and after the mid century, chairs in versions of the Chippendale style could be found as far apart as Philadelphia, Lisbon, Christiania (now Oslo) and Venice, and by the end of the century the styles of Adam, Hepplewhite and Sheraton had even wider influence. After 1780 Scandinavia was swept by a veritable 'anglomania' in which English chair design played a very important part. Foreign chair-makers came to London to complete their training; back home they and their fellows were helped by the flow of imported chairs from England and the publication of pattern books by English designers.

EARLY GEORGIAN: THE PRE-CHIPPENDALE ERA, 1714–50

The curvilinear chair continued to be made in the early years of George I's reign (1714–27), but it gradually lost its graceful simplicity. About 1720 more ornate decoration came into use, and chairs were distinctly heavier and more solid, with wider seats and lower backs. The splat was widened and sometimes connected to the uprights with volutes. Arm supports no longer continued directly upwards from the front legs but were set back on the side rails, and the arms, curved and 'dished' (i.e. flattened at a slight angle for the elbows), scrolled over the supports.

The backs of upholstered chairs and of winged armchairs were also reduced in height, and their legs took on cabriole form. Cabriole legs were now universal on all types of fashionable chairs, and stretchers were not used again until the revival of the straight leg in the middle of the century. Rich materials remained in demand for upholstery, with an increasing emphasis on comfort.

Wide circular and oval seats and splayed arms were necessary for comfortable sitting as fashionable costume at this time achieved extraordinary width. The hooped dresses worn by ladies, already wide, acquired greater width at the sides c. 1730–35 and extended even further in the next decade. Men too, needed plenty of chair room, for their coats stretched out in wide flared skirts which were often stiffened with buckram or whalebone.

In the second quarter of the century chair-making began to be affected by the introduction of mahogany, which was already known in Stuart England, but had not hitherto been used for furniture. An Act of Parliament of 1721, with the aim of increasing supplies of timber for the navy, abolished the heavy import duties on timbers from the British colonies in North America and the West Indies. The consequent fall in prices naturally encouraged merchants to exploit West Indian cabinet woods, of which mahogany was the chief. The main source of supply was Jamaica, which exported not only her own wood, but also mahogany from the Spanish islands of San Domingo, Cuba and Puerto Rico. The value of mahogany imports in England rose (at the official rate of £7 per ton) from a mere £277 in 1722 to almost £30,000 in 1750. The new wood appears for the first time in the royal furniture accounts in 1724 and was first used for chair-making c. 1725.

The Act of 1721 had put into the hands of English craftsmen a superb material, the like of which they had not used before. 'Spanish' wood, as this early mahogany was called, was hard, dark, close-grained, of almost metallic strength, impervious to attack

32. George I walnut side chairs with burr walnut veneers on the splats. The drop-in seats are upholstered with contemporary needlepoint.

by woodworm, and capable of taking a fine polish (*illus. 35*). It could also be carved with remarkable vigour and crispness.

It was not, however, until *c.* 1750 that mahogany could claim to have finally superseded walnut as the most fashionable wood. In fact, until that date probably as much furniture was made of walnut as of mahogany, but far less of the walnut has survived owing to its perishable nature.

Early mahogany chairs resembled in every way their walnut counterparts, but, as Spanish mahogany had little figure and was used in the solid and not as a veneer, its somewhat austere appearance was soon relieved by carved decoration, which gradually replaced the matched veneers of the walnut period. Splats now began to be pierced (*illus. 34*).

The years 1720–35 are sometimes known as the 'lion period' because many chairs of high quality had a lion's mask carved on the arms or on the front legs, which ended in lion's paw or paw-

33. Side chair of *c.* 1720 in the Saloon at Erddig Park in Wales, owned by the National Trust. This late 17th-century house has been extensively restored, and contains much of the original furniture. The cabriole legs and seat rails are carved with acanthus leaves and gilded; it is upholstered in the original Spitalfields crimson velvet.

34. Mahogany armchair of *c.* 1740, with pierced splat and arms terminating
in the lion mask.
35. An early example in mahogany of *c.* 1740, this chair of 'Spanish' wood has
an unusual form of rear legs suggesting a north-of-England origin.

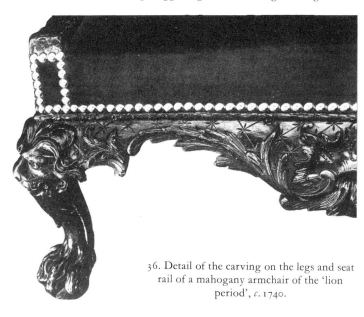

36. Detail of the carving on the legs and seat
rail of a mahogany armchair of the 'lion
period', *c.* 1740.

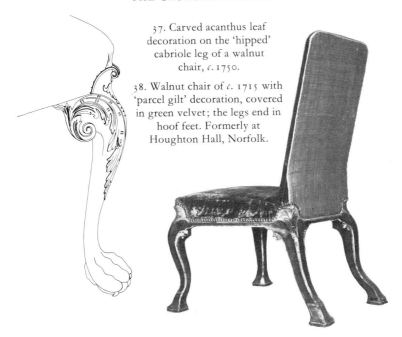

37. Carved acanthus leaf decoration on the 'hipped' cabriole leg of a walnut chair, *c.* 1750.

38. Walnut chair of *c.* 1715 with 'parcel gilt' decoration, covered in green velvet; the legs end in hoof feet. Formerly at Houghton Hall, Norfolk.

and-ball feet (*illus. 34, 36*). Some legs were realistically carved all over with the animal's hair. Almost as widely used, however, was the eagle motif, and legs were also carved with the cabochon (an oval jewel), leaves, and human or satyr masks. The splat, top rail and apron piece (the ornamental member below the centre of the front seat rail) were other decorated areas. The ends of scrolled arms were sometimes carved with eagles' heads. Some cabriole legs were 'hipped' – i.e. extended upwards to join the seat rail, a feature which became particularly popular for about twenty years after 1730 (*illus. 29 Left, 37*).

Chairs of exceptional quality were made of mahogany 'parcel-gilt' (i.e. with gilt enrichments) or were completely gilded. In the latter case the gold leaf was applied on a ground of gesso, a composition of chalk and parchment size which covered the framework (usually of a cheaper wood) and was carved in low relief (*illus. 33*). The first half of the century was the great age of gesso-gilding, which reached its height *c.* 1730. Silvering was also used but on a lesser scale.

Among the most lavishly decorated chairs of this period were

39. Armchair of *c.* 1740 with the carved and gilt gesso ornament of the Kent period.

40. Vitruvian scroll, a favoured classical motif of the Kent period; from the seat rail of a mahogany chair, *c.* 1730.

those designed by William Kent (1685–1748), the first English architect to include furniture as an integral part of his interior decoration. Under the patronage of the Earl of Burlington, Kent favoured the regular classical proportions of the Palladian revival for the exteriors of his houses, but filled the interiors with versions of the baroque furniture which he had seen in Italy, where he had studied painting from 1710 to 1719. He used much gilded and parcel-gilt ornament (as can be seen today in his chairs at Houghton Hall, Norfolk, made for Sir Robert Walpole), with lion and human masks, elaborate crestings, the double shell (a favourite device, set beneath the seat rails), acanthus scrolls, and repeated classical motifs, all combined with sumptuous and brightly coloured upholstery. But the furniture, though perfectly at home in its proper setting, has a monumental character which Horace Walpole, an admirer in general of Kent's work, described as 'often unmeasurably ponderous' (*illus.* 39).

English japanners were very active in the early decades of the century as Parliament had imposed additional duties on imported oriental lacquered goods, following a complaint by London furniture-makers that the imports threatened both their home manufacturers and the export of English furniture. Giles Grendey of Clerkenwell, joiner and chair-maker, is known to have exported japanned chairs on a large scale. A celebrated set from his workshop, consisting of a day-bed, six armchairs and 20 single chairs, all in brilliant red japan, has been found in Spain with his label on one of the armchairs.

In the Palladian houses of early Georgian England the library replaced the long gallery and this no doubt explains the introduction in this period of various kinds of reading and writing chairs. They were often made with three legs at the front and one at the back. Some had two splats and a semicircular top rail (*illus.* 41).

Others, sometimes known as 'library chairs', were made with padded arms and backs on which the occupant, sitting astride facing the rear, could rest his arms; a small desk for reading and writing was also attached to the back for his use. This type has sometimes been called a cock-fighting chair and it may possibly

41. Walnut writing chair of *c.* 1735, with curved uprights and pierced splats.

have been used in a cockpit, but its main function is obvious (*illus. 100*).

Hall chairs were also introduced at this time in the entrance halls and passages of larger houses, for the use of servants and tradesmen. They were usually made in sets, of mahogany, with solid backs, and were never upholstered (*illus. 99*).

CHIPPENDALE AND THE ROCOCO, *c.*1750–65

It took mahogany about a quarter of a century after its introduction to make a revolutionary impact on the structure as well as the

42. Walnut chair of *c.*1750, with gilt enrichments and splat in the form of an openwork shell.

43. Mahogany chair of *c.*1750, with openwork splat and key pattern on the seat rail.

decoration of chairs. About 1745 significant changes in the design of many chairs was becoming apparent (*illus. 42, 43*). The solid splat was now being pierced with tracery, scrolls and strapwork, the hoop shape was being replaced by almost vertical uprights which met the top rail in a tapering outward curve, and straight legs were beginning to return to favour. These changes indicated the earliest influence of the French rococo style which, in reaction against the massive baroque, found expression in light and delicate ornament in C and S scrolls, often in asymmetrical form. In England the rococo, suitably transplanted, had its greatest influence on furniture, and for this the credit is due to Thomas Chippendale (1718–79), the most celebrated name in English (and perhaps world) furniture. Chippendale's fame rests on the publication in 1754 of his pattern book, *The Gentleman and Cabinet-Maker's Director*, which provided wealthy clients and craftsmen with a complete guide, in 160 plates, to the latest furniture fashions. It was an immediate success, being reissued in 1755 and in a final edition (enlarged to 200 plates) in 1762. It was the first pattern book to be devoted to the complete range of domestic furniture, and the first to be published by a cabinet-maker. It was thought at one time that Chippendale employed two commercial artists, Lock and Copland, to produce the original drawings for the plates, which all bear his signature, but the available evidence points very strongly to his personal responsibility.

The publicity which the *Director* has given to Chippendale has perhaps unfairly obscured the names of some of his outstanding contemporaries, such as Vile and Cobb, the royal craftsmen, for although he had a large business in St Martin's Lane, then the chief cabinet-making centre of London, and had many distinguished patrons, he never succeeded in obtaining a royal appointment. As head of a busy firm he did not himself make furniture, and only a relatively few pieces are known with certainty to have come from his workshop. His name is therefore not a maker's label but a very convenient term for describing the mid-century styles which he popularised.

The predominant style of the *Director* is the English version of the rococo, then called the 'modern taste'. Chippendale added a few designs in the Chinese and Gothic styles, shrewdly perceiving that there was a revival of interest in *chinoiserie* (which was stimu-

44. Giltwood armchair upholstered in red figured silk; it was designed by
Robert Adam in 1764 and executed by Thomas Chippendale. Victoria and
Albert Museum, London.

45. Mahogany chair of *c.* 1760, with splat carved with Gothic tracery; the front legs are decorated with low relief frets and the stretchers with pierced frets.

46. (*Right*) A good example of a mahogany chair in the Chippendale style, *c.* 1765.

47. Mahogany chair in the Chinese taste, *c.* 1760; back filled with lattice-work; pagoda cresting; legs turned in imitation of bamboo.

lated by the publication of travel books on China) and that the Gothic decoration introduced by Horace Walpole at Strawberry Hill *c.* 1750 was being much admired in fashionable society. Both these subsidiary styles blended harmoniously with the English form of the rococo.

The success of the *Director* was infectious. It was soon followed by similar pattern books with the same style of design, including Ince and Mayhew's *Universal System of Household Furniture* (1759–62) and, more specialised, Robert Manwaring's *The Cabinet and Chair-Maker's Real Friend and Companion* (1765) and the same author's *Chair-Maker's Guide* (1766). Versions of 'Chippendale' chairs were found not only throughout England, but also in America and many parts of Europe.

The 1762 edition of the *Director* had 25 plates of chairs and other seats, totalling over 60 designs. Of the latter, 24, simply entitled 'chairs' or 'chair backs', represented the English translation of the rococo. In addition, French, Chinese, Gothic, 'ribband-back', garden and hall varieties were illustrated. The typical rococo chair had a pierced and interlaced splat, with carved scrollwork in varied light and fanciful forms which only mahogany could execute, uprights curving gently outwards, and a top rail of 'cupid's bow' shape (*illus.* 45, 46). The more extravagant rococo taste was exhibited in the 'ribband-back' chairs in which the splats were carved to represent interwoven silk ribbons. Only three designs for these chairs were given in the book.

'For the greater choice' of prospective buyers and makers, many of the chair designs showed two different front legs and back uprights, giving them a somewhat strange appearance. The front leg could be straight (and tapered) or of attenuated, delicately carved cabriole form, no longer ending on the claw-and-ball foot, but usually on a scroll, turning either outwards ('French scroll') (*illus.* 51) or inwards ('knurl' foot) (*illus.* 23). Stretchers, out of fashion for half a century, were reintroduced on chairs with straight legs. They were unnecessary from the structural point of view, particularly on mahogany chairs.

For the upholstery of his rococo chairs Chippendale writes that 'the Seats look best when stuffed over the Rails and have a Brass Border neatly chased; but are most commonly done with Brass Nails, in one or two Rows'.

48. Pair of Chippendale armchairs in the Chinese taste. Open fret-work supports the oval pad inset in the back, while blind fret-work decorates the flat surfaces. Although the upholstery is modern, the chairs retain their original decoration in off-white with traces of gilt.

Chippendale's Chinese chairs had backs completely made up of lattice-work (or 'railing') in geometric patterns (*illus. 47, 48*). The top rail was either straight or curved, in one case centring in a pagoda motif. The front legs were straight in every example. They were left plain or were decorated with pierced or low-relief frets, and had a fret-cut bracket in the angles with the front seat rail. The *Director*'s notes state that such chairs 'are very proper for a Lady's Dressing-Room: especially if it is hung with India Paper. . . . They have commonly Cane-Bottoms, with loose Cushions; but, if required, may have stuffed Seats and Brass Nails.' The Chinese taste was considered very suitable for bedrooms; and chairs were also japanned and had legs made to imitate bamboo (*illus. 47*). The firm of Linnell probably supplied the furniture for the well-known Chinese bedroom at Badminton, the home of the Duke of Beaufort, in *c*. 1750, including the japanned chairs with lattice backs.

49. Walnut armchair by Goudin (*le jeune, maitre-ebeniste*, 1752); this French type strongly influenced contemporary English chairs (*see* below).

50. Carved mahogany armchair of *c.* 1765, illustrating English devotion to French fashions.

51. Mahogany stool of *c.* 1765; carved acanthus leaves on the cabriole legs which end in 'French scroll' feet.

The *Director*'s 'Gothick' chairs were much less happy designs, hardly conforming to the attractive delicacy which was the distinguishing feature of 'Strawberry Hill Gothic'. The treatment of the rectangular backs tended to repeat the lattice-work of Chinese chairs, with rococo trimmings. Other Gothic chairs of the period were more successful when they had interlaced rococo backs incorporating delicate pointed arches or cusping (*illus.* 45).

Chippendale's 'French' chairs were upholstered armchairs. Two of his designs show plain upholstered backs, but the eight others are more elaborate versions, with strong rococo influence in the carved scrollwork on the curved back frames, the slender cabriole legs, the graceful arm supports and the seat rails. Some, according to the notes, were 'intended to be open below at the Back: which makes them very light, without have a bad Effect'. Such chairs had a space between the rear seat rail and the back, and, indeed, were very similar to contemporary French armchairs. French taste continued to exercise a dominating influence on England at this time (*illus. 49, 50*), and Chippendale himself is known to have imported French chair frames to finish in his workshop, for in 1769 he was fined by the Customs for failing to declare the correct value of sixty such frames.

Rococo chairs certainly combined comfort and elegance with a lightness of line which was in strong contrast to the ponderous chairs of the Kent period. The 'serpentine line, or line of grace', as William Hogarth, the famous artist, described it in his *Analysis of Beauty* in 1753, was the most characteristic feature of fashionable English chairs of the mid century. In 1757 Caroline Girle (the future Mrs Philip Lybbe Powys) was amused by the heavy Tudor furniture which she saw at Hardwick Hall, and she comments in her diary: 'I'm certain, if any one was to compare three or four hundred years hence a chair from the drawing-room of Queen Elizabeth's days and the light French ones of George II it would never be possible to suppose them to belong to the same race of people, as the one is altogether gigantic and the other quite lilliputian.'

'COUNTRY' CHAIRS

So far attention has been concentrated on the most fashionable chairs made after 1660, for it is only by a study of these, which were made in London, the country's chief furniture centre, by the most skilled craftsmen using the best available materials, that we can trace the chronology of the evolution of styles. It was customary for the aristocracy and many of the landed gentry in all parts of the country to send to London for their best furniture, in spite of the risk of damage to the goods in their often prolonged journeys by land or sea.

It would, however, be altogether misleading to divide English furniture into two broad categories of 'London' and 'country', the one setting and the other following the fashion. This over-simplification has been made so often that it has led to a serious neglect of the study of the regional characteristics of English furniture. An American scholar, John T. Kirk ('Sources of some American Regional Furniture', *Antiques*, December, 1965), has assembled impressive evidence relating regional differences in early American furniture to various areas of England. As it would appear natural for craftsmen among English emigrants to take their local methods of construction and decoration across the Atlantic with them, the whole subject obviously requires the attention of English students.

Outside London the standards of chair-making varied considerably. The principal provincial towns could produce work of good quality for the local squires and professional classes. The chairs, for instance, in the elegant Assembly Rooms at York, which was built in 1731–2 to the designs of the Earl of Burlington, were supplied by local craftsmen, as the Directors' Minute Book shows. The Purefoy family of Shalstone Manor, near Buckingham, whose papers have been preserved, bought furniture and upholstery from London, but also, in 1736, ordered some twenty chairs 'of walnut-tree frames with 4 legs without any Barrs' (i.e. stretchers) from a chair-maker named King at nearby Bicester. Away from market towns, in rural areas where, at least until the end of the 18th century, poor roads often meant comparative isolation, traditional methods of chair-making continued, only faintly and belatedly affected by changes in fashion.

In really remote districts there was little scope for specialisation. 'A country carpenter', writes Adam Smith in 1776 in his famous *Wealth of Nations*, 'deals in every sort of work that is made of wood. . . . [he] is not only a carpenter, but a joiner, a cabinet-maker and even a carver.' Primitive conditions lingered on in some areas into the next century. In his *Journal of a Tour and Residence in Great Britain, 1810–11*, Louis Simond, a Frenchman long resident in the United States, describes the furniture in Devon cottages as no more than 'a few seats, in the form of short benches – a table or two – a spinning wheel – a few shelves'. Furniture was often made at home; and not always in humble cottages, for at Townend in the Lake District, the home of a substantial yeoman family, the furniture, including many seats, still intact, was mostly made by successive generations of the family.

The country chair-maker who furnished cottages, farmhouses and inns made various kinds of joined, turned, spindle-back, stick-back and ladder-back chairs, using local woods such as oak, ash, beech, walnut, elm, yew and fruit woods. He might glimpse something of the latest fashions when he was called in to the local mansion to do repair work or supply chairs for the kitchen. In time, he might incorporate some small detail of what he had seen in his own chairs. The pattern books which appeared in the second half of the century, following Chippendale's *Director*, helped to shorten the interval between the emergence of a new style and its impact on country chairs.

In one respect the trend was reversed. That traditional country chair, the ladder-back, climbed up into the fashionable world in the Chippendale period. It was made into an elegant piece, the rungs of the ladder, sometimes pierced and carved, taking on a serpentine shape to fit the rococo taste.

WINDSOR CHAIRS

The most famous of all stick-back chairs is the Windsor, which is still made today in its traditional form as it emerged towards the end of the 17th century. The name 'Windsor' is a mystery. There is nothing to connect the chairs especially with the town of Windsor, and certainly nothing to substantiate the old story that they acquired their name when George III had a set made for Windsor Castle after seeing and admiring some in a cottage on his estate while sheltering from the rain. The name was in use long before George became king. The earliest reference so far recorded (quoted in A. M. Amherst's *History of Gardening in England*, 1895) is in 1724, when Lord Percival describes in a letter how his wife was carried 'in a Windsor chair like those at Versailles' in the garden of Hall Barn, Buckinghamshire. Other references to Windsor chairs in the 1720s (including the Royal Household accounts) make it clear that the name had wide currency by that time.

The earliest type of Windsor chair was the comb-back, which is named after the shaped top rail supported on sticks (*illus. 52*). The hoop-back, with its bent bow back into which the sticks

52. Windsor chair, elm, of comb-back type, the under-framing much worn; first half of the 18th century.

are socketed, came into use after 1750 and is a more familiar form, although it has never superseded the comb-back (*illus. 104*). These light and inexpensive chairs were commonly found in cottages, farmhouses, taverns, tea-gardens, smaller town houses, and also in the kitchens and servants' quarters of larger houses. Those intended for outdoor use were painted or stained, usually green.

Various woods were used in their manufacture, but elm was almost universally employed for the seat (which was given a saddle shape). Beech was favoured for the sticks, legs and stretchers, and ash or yew for bentwood members. Their construction was turner's work and not true joinery, for the square-cut mortise and tenon was very rarely used. The round turned legs were socketed into holes bored underneath the seat, and similarly the sticks for the back were fitted in holes bored in the top of the seat. The auger for boring and the draw-knife and spokeshave for shaping were the principal tools. The bentwood members, after first being prepared to the required size and section, were steamed (or soaked in water) to make them pliable, and then levered into shape and clamped until dry, when they retained their curved form.

Both the comb-back and hoop-back incorporated splats and cabriole legs, the latter having pad feet and, unlike those on fashionable chairs, stretchers. On armchairs a horizontal hoop often formed a semicircle across the back and along to the front as arm supports. The back sticks passed through this hoop, which was supported at the sides by sticks from the seat. All members of the chair were set at an angle, the legs and arm supports being splayed and the sticks raked outwards. From the 1750s the side stretchers were sometimes united by a curved stretcher. For extra strength two stays forming a brace might be found fixed from the top of the back to a small platform or bob-tail projecting from the rear of the seat.

The design of the chair was dictated by its method of construction, and decoration was confined to the turning or to the piercing of the splat. The cabriole leg was often of clumsy appearance, and its union with the clean functional lines of the back and seat was not always happy. Many splats had motifs inspired by fashionable decoration. Some fine examples made after 1750 had, instead of sticks in the back, a series of splats pierced with Gothic tracery. Later in the century the wheel and Prince of Wales's feathers were also found.

Mahogany Windsors were occasionally made for larger houses. The inventory of the Duke of Cumberland's furniture at Windsor Great Lodge in 1765 includes 'one mahogany elbow Windsor chair' in the butler's pantry.

Cheap varieties of Windsors were extensively advertised by the London warehouses, which did not make their own furniture but bought it from working masters. Wilkinson and Sons, for instance, advertised 'cabriole, japan'd, dyed and Windsor chairs' at their Cheapside warehouse in 1779.

Daniel Defoe writes in his *Tour through the Whole Island of Great Britain* (1724–26) that 'beech wood . . . grows in the woods of Buckinghamshire more plentifully than in any other part of England', and this area, with Chepping (now High) Wycombe as its centre, became particularly associated with the making of Windsor chairs, though they continued to be made in many other districts. In the beech woods of the Chilterns the turners, known locally as 'bodgers', prepared the legs and spindles of the chairs on their pole lathes, and other village craftsmen made seats, bows and splats. High Wycombe gradually became the centre for assembling the chair parts and dispatching them to London, the neighbouring counties and the Midlands, and it is still today the centre of a great chair-making industry.

A distinct regional type called the Mendlesham chair had a seat and turned legs like the Windsor, and a back of square or rectangular shape, with a straight top rail, vertical spindles, and turned balls in the space between the top and a cross rail. This type is said to have been originally made by Daniel Day of Mendlesham, Suffolk, and may thus be justifiably regarded as the East Anglian variety of Windsor.

Windsor chairs associated with the northern counties during the Georgian period show more elaborate turning than their southern counterparts, and are often made entirely of yew, except for the elm seat. In 1833 J. L. Loudon in his *Encyclopaedia of Cottage, Farm and Villa Architecture and Furniture* describes the Windsor as 'one of the best kitchen chairs in general use in the midland counties of England', and illustrates a bow-back example with a perforated splat of somewhat coarse design. He adds that the chairs are frequently stained 'a sort of red, not unlike mahogany', one method to achieve this effect being to lay slaked quicklime on the wood while hot – 'the general practice with the Windsor chair manufacturers in the neighbourhood of London'. In Wycombe at this time, on the other hand, the chairs were sold without stain or paint and were known as 'White Wycombes'.

The Windsor was transplanted to the American colonies early in the 18th century and was widely used there. A number of centres for their manufacture sprang up, notably Philadelphia, but, as in England, they were made in all parts of the country. The numerous local variations have been carefully analysed and classified by American students.

ADAM, HEPPLEWHITE AND THE NEO-CLASSICAL, *c.* 1765–90

When the rococo style went out of fashion in the 1760s, English furniture design was dominated for 50 years by classical taste. In the generation after the final edition of the *Director* the outstanding figure was the architect Robert Adam (1728–92), who developed the neo-classical style, a revival of classical forms in a

53. President's chair, Royal Society of Arts; designed by Sir William Chambers in 1759.

light and attractive interpretation. These forms, which caught something of the rococo, were applied with remarkable harmony to the whole field of architecture, interior decoration and furniture.

Recent research has modified in two respects traditional views of Adam's role as a designer. For long it has been held that he originated the neo-classical style as a result of his studies of ancient and Renaissance architecture in Italy and Dalmatia. It is now known that two architects, James Stuart and Sir William Chambers, preceded him in designing English neo-classical furniture. The President's chair of the Royal Society of Arts which Chambers designed in 1759 is considered to be the first neo-classical piece made in England (*illus. 53*). Important developments were also occurring at this same time in France in neo-classical decoration, and until conclusive evidence turns up it is as yet uncertain whether England or France can claim to be the birthplace of the new style.

It has always been assumed, too, that Adam designed all the furniture which was such an integral part of his decorative schemes, but it has recently been shown (Eileen Harris, *The Furniture of Robert Adam*, 1963) that much of this 'Adam' furniture was in fact designed in his style by the various firms, including Chippendale's, which were commissioned to furnish his houses. Among the many

54. Adam armchairs from a set of eight, and settee, of *c.* 1776. Tapestry Room, Osterley Park House, London.

original designs by Adam in the Soane Museum, London, only a relatively few are of furniture, and these are mainly pieces intended to be against or on the wall, which Adam would naturally design to complete his decoration of the room. One can no longer accept the view that Adam sent designs of furniture to his cabinet-makers who failed to return them. The craftsmen can now be credited with their own designs, much to the enhancement of their status, though they were obviously influenced by Adam's ideas. Chippendale showed an amazing mastery of the Adam style in which his firm produced their best pieces (*illus.* 44).

The very few chair designs by Adam himself include a set executed for Osterley Park House, Middlesex, and repeated more elaborately for a house in Hill Street, London. These are of carved and gilded wood with tapered fluted legs and a back of oval shape supported by winged sphinxes. This type closely followed French chair styles (*illus.* 54). Also at Osterley are some mahogany lyre-back chairs probably made by John Linnell to Adam's design. The lyre-back was one of the important contributions made by

75

55. Gilt armchair of *c.* 1775, with neo-classical decoration; oval back in the French taste; unusual combination of straight fluted front legs and cabriole rear legs.

England to European chair design. So too were the heart- and shield-shape backs which gave other chairs of the neo-classical period an elegant lightness. They were decorated with finely carved or inlaid classical ornaments such as the honeysuckle, pendant husks, draperies, urns, paterae, wheat-ears, etc., all carefully related to structural lines (*illus. 56, 57*).

The neo-classical style, which Adam developed for rich clients, was translated into general furniture by George Hepplewhite, whose name is used to describe the taste of *c.* 1770–1790. Hepplewhite, an obscure cabinet-maker of Cripplegate, London, is associated with *The Cabinet-Maker and Upholsterer's Guide*, which was published in 1788, two years after his death, by 'A. Hepplewhite & Co.' – presumably his widow, Alice, who continued his business. Though it is uncertain how far Hepplewhite himself was responsible for the 126 plates (which bear no name) illustrating nearly 300 designs, the pattern book was the best that had been published for 20 years; it was reissued in 1789 and, revised, in 1794.

Hepplewhite disclaimed originality, his purpose, declared in the preface, being to follow 'the latest or most prevailing fashion'. He

56. Carved oval patera on the cresting of a set of chairs designed by Robert Adam for Osterley in 1777.

57. Painted patera from the knee of a chair, c. 1780–85.

did not invent the oval, heart and shield shapes which figure in the chair designs in the *Guide*, though they are often credited to him. He may possibly, however, have been the first to have used the familiar Prince of Wales's feathers as a chair decoration. His designs were freely adapted by chair-makers and few seem to have been copied closely (*illus. 58, 59*). No chair or any other piece of furniture from his workshop has ever been identified.

The *Guide* sets out the general dimensions of chairs as: 'Width in front 20 inches, depth of seat 17 inches, height of the seat frame 17 inches, total height about 3 feet 1 inch'; but these could be adapted to the size of the room or the purchaser's wishes. Chair legs are usually straight and tapered, of either round or square section, the latter often ending on a plinth (or spade) foot. Except in one design, stretchers are not used. The first edition illustrates cabriole legs of attenuated form with 'French scroll' feet on 'chairs of state', but in the third edition only stools have cabriole legs and these are without scrolled feet. As already noted, the term 'cabriole' was applied at this time, somewhat confusingly, to chairs with stuffed backs.

In good mahogany chairs decorative mouldings were worked

58. Square-back armchair in mahogany, the splat with the Prince of Wales's feathers, similar to a design dated 1787 in Hepplewhite's *Guide* (1788).

59. Shield-back armchair of *c.* 1790 with painted decoration.

in the framework and fillings of the back, which was of concave shape. The *Guide*'s description is 'bars and frame in a hollow, or rising in a round projection, with a band or list on the inner and outer edges'. Such chairs, it is suggested, should have 'seats of horsehair, plain, striped, chequered, etc., at pleasure'. The notes in the *Guide* refer to the 'new and very elegant fashion' of japanning, and recommend that japanned or painted chairs should have cane seats and a lighter framework than was requisite for mahogany. This framework was commonly of beech. The cushions should have linen or cotton cases 'to accord with the general hue' of the chair.

60. Upholstered settee of *c.* 1785 with painted decoration in the Hepplewhite style.

61. Mahogany English *bergère* chair in the French taste, *c.* 1780.

The third edition of the *Guide* shows a significant revision of the earlier chair designs by increasing the number with square backs already represented in the first edition (*illus.* 58). Some of these are 'suitable for mahogany or japan'. For others, backs and seats of red or blue morocco, or backs incorporating medallions of printed or painted silk, are recommended. This change may well have resulted from Sheraton's criticism (in the preface to his *Drawing-Book*, 1791–4) that a comparison of Hepplewhite's designs, 'particularly the chairs', with those in the newest taste, suggests that the *Guide* 'has already caught the decline'. This square type was extensively used in the last decade of the century.

Other seats illustrated in the *Guide* include mahogany or japanned stools made *en suite* with chairs, window stools with two raised ends, settees with backs either upholstered (*illus. 60*) or of chair ('bar-back') form, hall chairs, a winged armchair, and the *duchesse* and *confidante*. The *duchesse* was a composite piece of two facing 'barjier' [*bergère* (*illus. 61*), or round-backed, easy] chairs with a stool between them, and the *confidante* was a settee with 'barjier' chairs set at an angle at each end.

Hepplewhite showed very considerable genius in the variety of his chairs. The oval- and particularly the shield-backs with their delicate classical ornament must rank among the most graceful achievements in the whole history of chair-making.

SHERATON, *c.*1790–1800

Important changes in taste occurred after *c.*1790. Emphasis was being increasingly laid on straight lines, extreme delicacy of form and, at first in fashionable circles, on close imitation of the furniture of the ancient world. In contrast to Adam's interpretation of classical ornament, furniture design was soon to become something of an archaeological pursuit. The long war with France (1793–1815) brought the need for economy, curtailed expensive methods of decoration and hastened the trend towards cheap, simple, useful and elegant furniture. Archibald Alison's *Essays on the Nature and Principles of Taste*, first published in 1790 and re-issued as late as 1825, reiterate the theme that, as Graeco-Roman furniture clearly shows, 'the greatest Delicacy which can be given to a Form is rather in the use of direct and angular Lines than in winding and serpentine ones', and that design should strive towards the 'last degree of Delicacy and Fragility'.

Delicate furniture, intended for middle-class homes, will always be associated with Thomas Sheraton (1751–1806), a journeyman cabinet-maker born in Stockton-on-Tees, who came to London in 1790 and eked out a poor living as an author and teacher of drawing. He does not seem to have had a workshop or made furniture to his designs, and freely admits that he found inspiration by touring the London furniture shops. Yet his pattern book, *The Cabinet-Maker and Upholsterer's Drawing-Book*, published in parts from 1791 to 1794, had some 700 subscribers (mainly in the trade)

62. Mahogany armchair of *c.* 1795, the back framework reeded with lattice-work filling.

63. Turned beech armchair of *c.* 1800, japanned in black and gold.

from all parts of England, and with its 113 plates of elegant designs displaying fine draughtsmanship and considerable fertility of invention, as well as its copious notes of explanation for craftsmen, achieved deserved popularity and, judging from the number of surviving pieces based on the designs, became widely influential. It was reissued in 1794 and 1802 and provides a valuable summary of the furniture of *c.* 1790–1800.

The chairs in the *Drawing-Book* have an almost feminine lightness, but the author was perfectly well aware of the consummate technical skill that was available (as perhaps at no other time in England) to make them. Most of those designated 'parlour' (i.e. dining-parlour) and 'painted' chairs have square backs (only two shield-backs are shown), their vertical lines accentuated by varied and original arrangements of bars (*illus.* 62) which are grouped in some instances into a central splat, and which are decorated with fashionable classical motifs. Top and bottom rails of the backs are normally straight and narrow. For parlour chairs mahogany is recommended. The designs for painted (and japanned) chairs are perhaps more fanciful, but differ only in detail from mahogany ones. Surviving japanned examples, in black or colour, are usually of beech with cane seats (*illus. 63*). The revival of cane-work seats was a refinement strongly advocated by Sheraton for both japanned chairs and mahogany parlour chairs which would look neat with small cane borders also round their backs.

Parlour chairs have straight-fronted seats; drawing-room chairs, on the other hand, have rounded or shaped upholstered seats and are 'finished in white and gold, or ornaments may be japanned'. Legs on all types of chairs are slender and tapering, and usually cylindrical (*illus. 62, 63*). An important new decoration is reeding, or convex ribbing, the reverse of the hollow fluting which it now supplants. Highly distinctive Sheraton touches can be seen in the graceful upward sweep of chair arms to meet the back near the top, and in the elegant slender scroll of the arms above their supports. It should be noted that though satinwood has often been associated with Sheraton, it was seldom used for chairs of this period.

'Conversation' chairs illustrated in the *Drawing-Book* have deep upholstered seats and padded top rails on which the sitters, facing backwards, could rest their arms as on the library and reading chairs. Other seats include two upholstered settees of somewhat severe lines, and two designs of a *chaise longue*, 'a long chair . . . to rest or loll upon after dinner'.

Sheraton's reputation rests firmly on the *Drawing-Book*, which bridged the interval between Adam and the Regency. He published two more books, *The Cabinet Dictionary* (1803) and an unfinished *Encyclopaedia* (1805). In neither do the designs equal the draughtsmanship and inventiveness of the *Drawing-Book*, and indeed those in the *Encyclopaedia* are eccentric to a degree. In the *Cabinet Dictionary*, however, besides much useful information, appear the first signs in an English publication of the Regency style.

REGENCY, *c.* 1800–30

The Regency style in furniture overlaps the political Regency of 1811–20, for it had its roots in the 18th century and lingered on after the end of the Georgian period. In the 1780s Adam's neo-classicism, as has been seen, was challenged by a revival of 'pure'

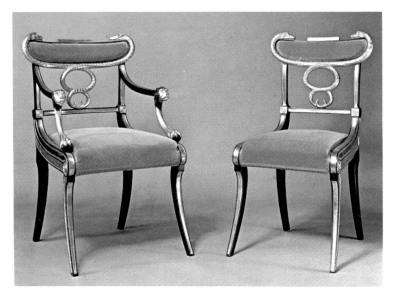

64. Regency chairs of *c.* 1810, from a very fine set consisting of two armchairs and two single chairs. Painted, with gilt enrichments, the arm-supports terminate in lions' heads and feet. The upholstered shoulder board is supported by entwined snakes. The legs are of sabre form.

classicism which, prompted by the archaeological study of antiquities, aimed to imitate closely the furniture of ancient Egypt, Greece and Rome. The pioneer of this new style in England was the architect Henry Holland (1751–1806), who began to rebuild Carlton House for the Prince of Wales in 1783. As the Prince and his Whig friends had pro-French sympathies, Holland's furniture, the design of which he must have supervised closely, was at first a blend of late Louis XVI classicism and Graeco-Roman styles (which became the Empire style in France). But it matured later into a truly English version, the Regency style, both at Carlton House and in other houses, notably Southill, which were re-furnished by Holland. The Prince and his circle also collected French furniture and employed French craftsmen.

Sheraton, who visited Carlton House in 1793, introduced features of the new style into his *Cabinet Dictionary*, including the first published English design of the Grecian couch with lion-paw feet and scrolled ends. 'Grecian severity' was one of the main trends in the classical revival, and 'Grecian' became a widely used (and abused) term among designers well into Victoria's reign. The strictly classical basis of the Regency was reaffirmed in Thomas Hope's *Household Furniture and Interior Decoration* (1807). Hope, a rich connoisseur and scholar, collected antiquities and made drawings of ancient remains during extensive travels in the eastern Mediterranean, and his book illustrates furniture in his London house which was made in imitation, or as skilful adaptation, of ancient pieces.

In addition to the French and various antique (including Etruscan) elements already apparent in Regency furniture, there was renewed interest in the Chinese and Gothic tastes for which the Chinese interior of Brighton Pavilion (enlarged in 1802) and the Romantic Revival in literature were largely responsible. All these features appear in the most comprehensive pattern book of the time, George Smith's *A Collection of Designs for Household Furniture and Interior Decoration* (1808). Smith, a cabinet-maker, standardised Regency taste for the trade by freely adapting designs from Sheraton, Hope and the French.

The discipline and scholarship of gifted men like Holland and Hope were gradually lost when their styles passed into general circulation. Austere classicism – itself often too rigid – could become indiscriminate application of antique motifs. Popular versions, for instance, of the Egyptian revival appeared after 1798, the year when Napoleon's Egyptian campaign was dramatically cut short by Nelson's victory at the Nile. Napoleon was accompanied by a team of scholars under D. V. Denon, whose researches, published in 1802, gave Europe accurate archaeological data of Egyptian antiquities. But in England Nelson's victory also made the revival something of a craze in which any emblem supposedly connected with Egypt might be found ornamenting furniture.

The Regency style, however, was too well founded on fine craftsmanship and good taste to hasten to a sudden decline. One of the lasting effects of the Greek revival was the resurrection of the *klismos* which was now skilfully interpreted to balance the continuous curve of the uprights and rear legs with the concave front legs. The result was a revolutionary change in English chair design. In strictly classical types the back had a broad concave

66. Beech armchair of *c.* 1825, carved and gilded, in the Gothic taste; upholstered in contemporary brown velvet with silk embroidery. Victoria and Albert Museum, London.

65. Painted and gilt armchair of *c.* 1810 with lion monopodia front legs and cane back and seat.

yoke ('arc-back') at shoulder level, but more usually it was of 'scroll-back' form, the uprights scrolling outwards and backwards to the top. One graceful version was the parlour chair which appeared shortly after 1800 and became known as the 'Trafalgar' chair (*illus. 103*). It has inward-curving ('sabre' or 'scimitar') front legs, which in the true sabre form are of oblong section narrower in the front than at the back, side rails making a continuous curve with the swept-back uprights, and outward-curving rear legs. Its light appearance is enhanced by a cane seat, on which a squab cushion is fastened from beneath, and by the simple filling (sometimes also cane) in the back. The top is either a shoulder board or a turned rail, often with a rope or cable moulding curved for the sitter's back. The material is normally beech, painted black or

67. Upholstered settee or sofa of *c.* 1805, carved and gilded, the legs formed as lion terminals. Formerly at Caledon, Co. Tyrone.

68. X-frame stool of *c.* 1810, carved and gilded.

bronze-green. Endless varieties of this kind of chair-back design can be found, but they nearly all emphasize horizontal lines, in contrast to the vertical trend of the neo-classical phase.

Drawing-room chairs were more elaborate, and were of mahogany, or were painted and gilt. In the early Regency, some fine gilt armchairs, influenced by French 'Etruscan' types (actually derived from Greek vase paintings) had strongly curved rear legs, scrolled uprights and arm supports, and straight or curved front legs (*illus.* 97). Some magnificent examples were made for Holland's houses. The arms of these 'Etruscan' chairs, where the downward sweep is balanced by the inward curve of the supports, represent one of the most elegant developments of the time. Another distinct Regency feature, common by 1805, was an even bolder scroll downwards and inwards to rest on the side rails of the seat.

Animal monopodia (lion or chimera heads with a single leg or foot) forming the front legs or arm supports of chairs were popularised by Sheraton and Smith (*illus. 64, 65*). Lion-paw feet were favourite terminals of front legs. The Egyptian taste was represented by a number of motifs, in which the sphinx and other Egyptian figures (*illus. 96*), and the lotus leaf ('the lily of the Nile') were prominent. 'Chinese' chairs were japanned and decorated with oriental motifs, and their legs were often made to imitate bamboo. Illustration 66 shows a 'Gothic' chair of the period.

Among the distinct chair types of the period were the curule, with crossed front legs based on the ancient *sella curulis* (*illus. 96*); the curricle, a tub-shaped chair for the library, so called by Sheraton after a carriage; the *bergère*, with caned back, sides and seat, the back and seat being occasionally cushioned (*illus. 95*); and the gondola or spoon-back.

The Grecian couch was particularly fashionable during the Regency through its associations with classical antiquity. It had one raised end, a short arm rest and a small scroll at the foot. Sheraton distinguished this kind from the sofa (though both couch and sofa descend from the day-bed) by giving the latter ends of equal height and a continuous high back (*illus. 67*). Settees, as always, followed chair evolution precisely (*illus 69*). Regency stools were especially attractive, and the cross-framed design, universally popular, must rank as one of the most graceful ever made in England (*illus. 68*).

69. Settee of *c.* 1805, with cane back and seat, painted black and gold.

CHAPTER SIX

Early Victorian
c. 1830-60

THE ARBITRARY selection of 1830 as the terminal date of 'antique' furniture has, until recently, created the impression that post-1830 furniture is not worth serious attention, and that the ornate furniture at the Great Exhibition of 1851 is typical (which it is not) of the time. Victorian furniture does not match Georgian stylistic standards, but much of it is well made from excellent materials, and increasing respect is paid to its outstanding designers. The Victorians lived in the new and rapidly changing world of the Industrial Revolution, when the long classical reign was ending in a reaction against Georgian 'uniformity'. In spite of areas of social distress, the general standard of living was rising. More families than ever before had homes of their own and the means to furnish them. The overriding consideration was comfort, which was now the most important element in chair design. 'Ease should be the great desideratum' is Richard Brown's verdict on dining-room chairs as early as 1820 (*Rudiments of Drawing Cabinet and Upholstery Furniture*), with the note that 'it now baffles the most skilful artist to produce new forms'. Seating furniture was generally covered with materials which were available in abundance from the factories, and comfort, not style, was the aim. The Victorian period might well be termed 'the age of the upholsterer'. Unfortunately, upholstery hid so much of the framework of seats that their former elegant outline was largely lost, and further deterioration occurred because the cheap furniture intended for the new mass market was often hurriedly made by the trade in poor imitation of the styles of competent designers.

The period produced a bewildering variety of styles, most of them already evident in the Regency. Loudon's *Encyclopaedia* (first published in 1833 and reissued as late as 1867) names, as the four fashionable styles of villa furniture, the Grecian (or modern),

70. Two dining-room chairs in the 'Grecian' style of the early Victorian period, from Thomas King's *Original Designs for Chairs, etc., c.* 1840.

Gothic, Elizabethan and Louis XIV. These had appeared in George Smith's *Cabinet-Maker's and Upholsterer's Guide* (1828) in which he states that his earlier work of 1808 was now obsolete and that chair design was suffering from 'a mixture of all the different styles associated together'. In 1847 Henry Whitaker's *Practical Cabinet Maker and Upholsterer's Treasury of Designs*, one of the best pattern books of the time, lists no fewer than seven fashionable styles: Grecian, Italian, Renaissance, Louis XIV, Gothic, Tudor and Elizabethan, to which he adds 'François Premier' and to which his contemporaries added Louis XV, Moorish, Pompeian and others. As art history was then in its infancy, these styles were rarely understood or clearly separated. According to the current theory of 'association of ideas', they were supposed to reflect, often romantically, the atmosphere of their period. In particular, the Gothic and Elizabethan were regarded as sturdy and truly national styles, their popularity owing much to antiquarian books such as Shaw's *Specimens*, 1836 (*see pp. 17 and 32*) and to Scott's historical novels.

71. 'Chairs in the Louis Quatorze style with stuffed backs and intended for the drawing-room,' from Henry Whitaker's *Practical Cabinet Maker and Upholsterer's Treasury of Designs*, 1847.

Of Loudon's four styles, Grecian chairs represented the last fling of classical tradition. The typical 'pseudo-*klismos*' or 'subclassical' dining chair had a broad horizontal yoke rail extending well beyond the uprights, slightly curved back legs, and turned straight front legs (which gradually ousted the swept legs). Purity of outline and ornament, by Regency standards, tended to coarsen, but some good examples, retaining much of the old elegance, were designed by the architect Philip Hardwick for the Goldsmiths' Hall in 1834, and other sets of the time are not without appeal, particularly when thickness in the front turned legs is avoided and they taper gracefully. Authors of pattern books, like Thomas King (*Original Designs for Chairs, etc., c.*1840), present endlessly varied treatment of the broad yoke rail – spiral volutes, rosettes, acanthus, etc., at the ends, carved ornaments in the centre, or merely plain wood – and of the filling between the yoke rail and seat – carved cross pieces (sometimes continued up to the top rail), narrow upholstery bands, or simply empty space (*illus. 70, 72*).

The Louis XIV (merging with the Louis XV) or 'Old French' style, was almost completely rococo in inspiration and was the only early Victorian revival influenced by the otherwise unfashionable 18th century (*illus. 71*). The Bourbon restoration of 1814

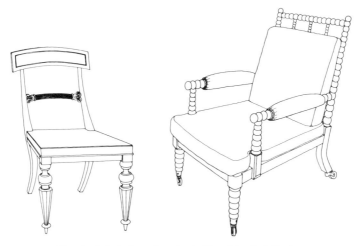

72. 'Grecian' chair from Loudon's *Encyclopaedia* (1833).

73. Easy chair of *c*. 1855–60 with turned frame and front legs.

renewed English taste for French fashions, and in the 1820s members of the architectural family of Wyatt redecorated several well-known houses in the Louis XIV manner. The trend was found in pattern books in the 1830s, such as Thomas King's *Modern Style of Cabinet Work Exemplified* (1835), in which 'the English style is carefully blended with the Parisian taste'. Old French chairs had, unlike other chairs of the time, backs of curvilinear form, elaborately carved with scrolls and volutes, and often lavishly gilded, as well as cabriole legs. They were favoured for drawing-rooms and boudoirs, and indeed their feminine lightness had an attraction which made them popular until the end of the century. A particularly light and elegant variety for ladies' apartments was known as a 'fly' chair; '12 fly chairs much ornamented' were regilded by Thomas Ponsonby, carver and gilder, for Buckingham Palace in 1855 for £9.

Elizabethan or 'high-back' chairs, normally made with spiral or baluster turning, are really nearly all late Stuart revivals, and not 'Elizabethan' at all (*illus. 75, 76*). Ackermann's *Repository of Arts* as early as 1817 illustrates an Elizabethan chair with spiral turned uprights and semicircular cresting, and Smith's *Guide* (1828) mentions the 'light spiral columns in the backs of chairs'. Some

74. 'Two drawing-room chairs with sweep back' from Thomas King's *Original Designs for Chairs, etc., c.* 1840. This type anticipated the early Victorian balloon-back.

attractive examples were designed by Anthony Salvin (1799–1881), architect and antiquarian, for Mamhead, Devon (1827–33), and Scotney Castle, Kent (1833–43), and a fine oak set of 24, with spiral turned uprights, legs and stretchers, the backs and seats upholstered in orange-red Genoa velvet, were made for Charlecote Park, Warwickshire, *c.*1835. Undoubtedly the cheapness of the turning as well as the romantic associations made the style popular. Henry Wood's *Useful and Modern Work on Chairs* (*c.*1845) and similar pattern books turned the Elizabethan high-back into the typical early Victorian drawing-room chair, some kinds having spiral uprights while others now had fully upholstered backs and cabriole legs. The high-back was still popular in the 1850s, as is shown in the designs in P. Thomson's *Cabinet-Maker's Sketchbook* (*c.*1855–60).

Early Victorian Gothic chairs had at first much in common with the romantic 'Gothick' of the Regency. They are recognised by their ornamental tracery, buttresses, pinnacles and crockets, applied to frames which are otherwise the same as those of Grecian chairs. A new and serious archaeological interpretation of Gothic, with a strong religious motive, was made by A. W. N. Pugin (1812–52), a convert to Roman Catholicism, in his publication of 1835, *Gothic*

Furniture of the 15th Century. Pugin designed furniture for the Medieval Court at the Great Exhibition, for a number of private clients (including some fine chairs for Scarisbrick Hall, Lancs), and for the rebuilt Houses of Parliament. Many of Pugin's chair designs have a simple vigour which may have been more generally influential than has been supposed; but by the 1840s Gothic chairs became heavier and more ornately carved, and manufacturers, even outstanding ones like J. G. Crace (with whom Pugin had collaborated), exploited his more elaborate designs after his death. Gothic chairs were almost always of oak, much of which (ironically enough, in view of this English national style) was imported from the Baltic.

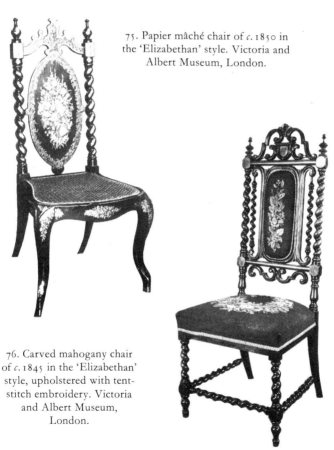

75. Papier mâché chair of *c.* 1850 in the 'Elizabethan' style. Victoria and Albert Museum, London.

76. Carved mahogany chair of *c.* 1845 in the 'Elizabethan' style, upholstered with tent-stitch embroidery. Victoria and Albert Museum, London.

77. Walnut drawing-room chairs of a balloon-back type, *c.* 1840.

The search for comfort introduced into chairs (as in furniture generally, in all the 'historic' styles) the important structural change of the curve, and this resulted in the development of the balloon-back chair (its modern, and not contemporary, name), one of the two original contributions of the period to English chair design (*illus. 74, 77, 94*). In the 1830s both the yoke rail of the Grecian type and the scroll-back of the Louis XIV were rounded off, as can be seen in the pattern books of the time. By *c.* 1850 the complete balloon-back, with cabriole legs for the drawing-room and straight legs for the dining-room, became universally popular. Though it has been said that there is no contemporary reference to this type, King's *Original Designs for Chairs*, etc. (*c.* 1840), shows two drawing-room examples quite clearly under the name of 'sweep back', and this name is also applied to a slender, cane-seated version in birch in a collection of pen drawings of *c.* 1840 (now in the Victoria and Albert Museum) by the well-known firm of W. Smee and Sons. These lighter 'sweep backs' were also termed 'fancy' or 'chamber' chairs.

The other original chair of the time was the *prie-dieu*, also known

78. Japanned chair of *c.* 1850, with cane seat and decorated with gilding and mother-of-pearl inlay. Victoria and Albert Museum, London.

as the 'vesper' or 'devotional' (and so called by Smee), with tall upholstered back, low seat and short legs. Some versions had elaborate turned uprights and legs, derived (like the Elizabethan) from late Stuart models, and these were intended for drawing-rooms. A specifically devotional type, with a T-shaped back and padded top-rest for family prayers, was popular c. mid century, and is shown in Henry Lawford's *Album Designs for Chairs* (c. 1855).

Chairs of papier mâché illustrate the Victorians' fondness for experimenting with materials other than wood. A fresh vogue for papier mâché began when Jennens and Bettridge of Birmingham, the chief makers, used it, often on a framework of wood or metal, for a wide range of furniture in the 1820s. The favourite method of decoration was to japan the smooth, hard surface black and then paint it with flowers or scenes in natural colours, embellished with gilding or pearl-shell inlay (*illus. 78, 101*). Such furniture has been frequently derided because of the ornate examples shown at the Great Exhibition, where one of the best known exhibits (often quoted to illustrate Victorian taste at its most questionable) was the 'Day Dreamer', an elaborately upholstered easy chair in papier mâché decorated with figures and emblems of sleep. Many chair-makers, however, used the material with skill and understanding, and, as well as producing light and attractive chairs, they made excellent use of its plastic qualities for moulded backs of *bergère* form.

After 1825 the most popular and ubiquitous of all the variants of the Windsor chair, the 'smoker's bow', appeared. Its low back and arms formed a horizontal semicircle which was supported from the seat by turned spindles (*illus. 102*). These sturdy, cheap and comfortable chairs, many of which are still in use today, were found not only in public smoking-rooms, but in cottages, in small houses in the expanding suburbs and in institutions of every kind. Other Windsors adhered to their traditional forms, suitably adapted to Victorian taste. A common kitchen version had a broad yoke like that of a Grecian chair, supported by sticks, spindles or laths. Windsor chairs were extensively used in the royal households; nearly a hundred were supplied to Buckingham Palace, Kew Palace and Windsor Castle between the end of 1855 and the early part of 1857 by W. Francis and W. Mealing. The basic simplicity of Windsors appealed strongly to reformist designers

79. Miniature chairs and stools depicting the characteristics of the Victorian easy chair with the buttoned and fringed upholstery of *c.* 1850–60. Victoria and Albert Museum, London.

of the 1860s. 'They are really superior in point of design to many pretentious elegances of fashionable make', writes Charles L. Eastlake (1836–1906) in his influential *Hints on Household Taste* (1868), in which he illustrates an example in the Gothic taste.

Rivalling Windsors in cheapness, comfort, simplicity and good design, though in this case of foreign origin, were the famous bentwood chairs made by the firm of Thonet. Michael Thonet (1796–1871), the Austrian cabinet-maker who founded the business, was a century ahead of his time in his methods of using steam power and standardised designs for the mass production of chairs, which were made at first of veneers bent in moulds under heat and later of solid bent beech wood. Thonet exhibited at the Great Exhibition, and by the 1860s his ingeniously constructed bentwood chairs were found in most Victorian households and in shops, hotels and similar buildings. His rocking chair was particularly popular.

The easy chair exemplifies the constant Victorian search for comfort, however much designers criticised its shape, and writers on etiquette its tendency to encourage the vice of lounging. Ever since Samuel Pratt's patent of 1828 for wire springs for beds, cushions, etc., deep-sprung, buttoned upholstery and short legs became typical features of this type of chair until the end of the century (*illus. 79*). After 1860 pioneer designers, well ahead of their time, sought to subordinate comfort to good style, but their contemporaries echoed Robert Kerr (*The Gentleman's House*, 1864) in calling 'a comfortable home the most cherished possession of an Englishman', in which the first consideration was comfort (for family and guests), then convenience (for servants) and finally elegance (without ostentation).

Another persistent Victorian practice was to give chairs and seats (and other pieces) fanciful names, usually with a romantic ring, which bore no relation to their actual use, and between which (except for a few generally accepted types) it is practically impossible to distinguish. About 1885, for instance, the catalogue of Howard and Sons of Berners Street, London, had some twenty different names for chairs and sofas. This firm also offered chairs in the Renaissance, François I, Henri II, Louis XV and Louis XVI styles – a reminder of the long vogue of some of these styles and the innate conservatism of much of Victorian taste.

A simpler form of upholstery, very fashionable after 1830 because it could be worked at home, was Berlin woolwork or cross-stitch embroidery in wool on open-meshed (later machine-woven) canvas. It was this work which undoubtedly made the *prie-dieu* so popular. But the upholsterer came into his own with the cushioning in a variety of materials, terminating in fringes down to floor level, on easy chairs and sofas (both types often had the back, arms and seats all sprung), circular and rectangular ottomans, pouffes (cylindrical seats without any visible woodwork), and various kinds of conversation seats, joined on an S-plan and so enabling people to sit facing each other, which went by the name of '*confidantes*', '*têtes-à-têtes*' or '*sociables*'.

CHAPTER SEVEN

Late Victorian and Edwardian
c. 1860–1914

AFTER 1860 a number of designers made determined efforts to improve standards of taste. Their work was at first appreciated by only a few, for most people were content with mass-produced furniture embodying ill-digested versions of styles interpreted by hack trade designers. One of the most influential designers (in the long run), though he had little personal interest in furniture, was William Morris (1834–96), who, with friends, founded a firm in 1861 (subsequently known as 'Morris & Co.') to produce articles of fine craftsmanship and good design. Morris made the two mistakes of over-praising medieval crafts (and scorning those of the Georgian period) and of disliking machinery (on which he laid the blame for the ugliness of his time). Much of his firm's furniture was too expensive for most homes. Nevertheless, Morris's influence made 'a chair, a wallpaper, or a vase a worthy object of the artist's imagination' (N. Pevsner, *Pioneers of Modern Design*, revised edition, 1960), and among the cheaper 'workaday' pieces of the firm, mainly designed by Philip Webb and Ford Madox Brown, were two deservedly famous chairs. One, the 'Sussex' chair, produced from *c.* 1865, was based on a rural type and had a rush seat and simple turned frame of birch or beech, stained black (*illus.* 98). This type was illustrated, with approval, in Robert E. Edis's *Decoration and Furniture of Town Houses* (1881), together with a plain bedroom chair by the same firm. The other (or 'Morris') chair, made from *c.* 1866, was an upholstered, long-seated easy chair with adjustable back, far lighter than most contemporary examples. This chair became very popular in the United States, where English furniture had a devoted following. Eastlake's book of 1868 was so widely read in both England and America that an 'Eastlake' style was developed, based on his 'Early English' version of Gothic furniture, of simple massive construction held together

80. Oak drawing-room chair covered with velvet and trimmed with a silk fringe, from C. L. Eastlake's *Hints on Household Taste* (1868).

(in medieval fashion) by pegged joints without glue. Illustration 80 shows a chair designed by Eastlake.

This led to the 'Art Furniture' movement of the 1870s and 1880s, which produced much well-designed and executed furniture before it was debased by the trade. The movement extended far beyond the Gothic, whose chief designers included W. Burges (1827–81) and B. J. Talbert (1838–81) as well as Eastlake, and also covered 18th-century revivals. Some chairs of the classic 1750–1800 period were so faithfully copied that, with a century's patination, they are now difficult to distinguish from their originals. Among many 'Art Furniture Manufacturers', Collinson and Lock of London were outstanding. They employed the gifted architect T. E. Collcutt (1840–1924) to design furniture in varied styles, and his dining chairs, with turned legs and stretchers, and a central back panel bounded top and bottom by rows of turned balusters, set the fashion for some twenty years. Another architect, E. W. Godwin (1833–86), was among the first in England to take an interest in Japanese crafts, which inspired his design of light, elegant and well-proportioned chairs quite different from their 'Early English' contemporaries, and forecasting a return to simple, graceful forms (*illus.* 82). This 'Anglo-Japanese' style degenerated into wholesale production of flimsy chairs of bamboo (genuine and imitation), and 'Art Furniture', merging into the 'Aesthetic Movement', was generally satirised (by Gilbert and Sullivan, among others, in *Patience*, 1881) in the 1880s.

A remarkable revival of handicraft, in which the influence of Morris was paramount, occurred after 1880 with the advent of the Arts and Crafts Movement. In 1882 the Century Guild founded by A. H. Mackmurdo (1851–1942) (*illus. 83*) was the first of a series of societies of craftsmen and designers formed to make fine furniture and publicise it through exhibitions. The furniture was not all of the simple early Morris type, for much of it (including Morris & Co.'s) was inspired by Queen Anne and Georgian models, and many chairs were 18th-century reproductions.

The early Morris tradition, however, was faithfully upheld by the 'Cotswold School', an offshoot of the new movement, in which the most important artist-craftsman was Ernest Gimson (1864–

81. Sussex chair, ebonised beech and rush seat; made by Morris & Co. from *c*. 1865. Victoria and Albert Museum, London.

82. Chair of ebonised wood, designed by E. W. Godwin and made by William Watt of London, 1885. Victoria and Albert Museum, London.

83. Dining-room chair of *c.* 1882 by A. H. Mackmurdo. The unusual fret-work back depicts tall sinuous flowers in the Art Nouveau style. Note that straight legs are still used for dining-room chairs. William Morris Gallery, Walthamstow.

84. Painted chair and table by Charles Rennie Mackintosh, *c.* 1900.
Mackintosh Collection, University of Glasgow.

1919). Inspired by Morris, Gimson, who had learnt the craft of chair-making from a rural Herefordshire craftsman, abandoned a career in architecture to set up a workshop with the Barnsley brothers in the Cotswolds in 1893. Gimson's other pieces (which he designed and did not make) were not all as superbly simple as his chairs. These were often rush-seated ladder-backs with elegant, slender, turned spindle legs, stretchers and uprights (which were continuations of the back legs) (*illus. 98*). He also designed some beautiful square-back chairs with vertical uprights. Gimson, who used a variety of native woods, had a wonderful feeling for materials, and it is due to him more than to anyone else that Morris's ideals, the traditions of English rural craftsmanship and the highest standards of hand skill have survived in English furniture right down to the present day.

The skills revived by the Arts and Crafts Movement were absorbed into a movement of quite different character (*illus. 85*). This was *Art Nouveau*, which, in spite of its name, owed much of its inception to England. It deliberately abandoned historical revivals to find a new art form for the 20th century, and it emphasised natural shapes based on vegetation, and expressed, wherever possible, in sinuous curves. Cheap commercial versions vulgarised these forms into what became known as the 'Quaint' style, but to condemn *Art Nouveau* unreservedly is to ignore the fact that much of its best furniture (which has aroused great interest recently) is well designed and well made. Of outstanding interest is the work of C. F. A. Voysey (1857–1941), the architect and designer, who was admired abroad as one of the chief inspirers of *Art Nouveau*. He was fond of the heart motif, which is found cut out on the backs of his chairs. The latter also display a typical structural feature of the style in that the uprights and front legs continue above the line of the top rail and seat, and sometimes end in small flat platforms. Voysey always used plain oak, unstained and unpolished, and the slender and elegant lines of his chairs (as of his furniture generally) made him a pioneer in the design of simple, uncluttered interiors.

Other features of the better chairs in this style were the low position of stretchers at almost ground level, and inlaid decoration in curved forms. Cheaper furniture was marred by the use of spindly legs, some armchairs requiring six for stability. The Scottish

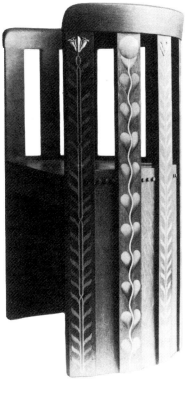

85. Carved oak chair with applied ornament; designed by M. H. Baillie Scott and made by the Guild of Handicraft for the Grand Duke of Hesse, 1898. Victoria and Albert Museum, London.

86. Ash armchair stained green, with rush seat; made by William Birch of High Wycombe, 1902. Nordenfjeldske Kuntindustrimuseum, Trondheim, Norway.

architect C. R. Mackintosh (1868–1928) designed some extraordinarily high-backed chairs (some up to five feet) but though much admired in Scotland and abroad, his work was little appreciated in England (*illus. 84*).

Ever since the 17th century English furniture had been exported to all parts of the world, and thousands of chairs found their way into colonial and foreign homes. This trade was at its peak in Victoria's reign, the total value of exported furniture in 1890, for instance, reaching the considerable sum (in wholesale prices) of almost £650,000. At that time British overseas territories naturally absorbed much of these exports, but the United States, the Argentine, and European countries such as Germany, France, Holland, Belgium and Spain were also very good customers. Furniture of the Arts and Crafts Movement was greatly admired abroad, and even when *Art Nouveau* flourished on the Continent its devotees there continued to regard Britain as their fountainhead and to import its furniture. Indeed, the work of some British designers was more highly appreciated abroad than at home. Yet this impressive and well-established trade represents in one way a missed opportunity. England failed to carry her leadership into the new Modern Movement of the 20th century, for pioneer work in industrial design and in experimenting with the new materials and techniques of industry passed into the hands of Germans, with the establishment of the Werkbund in 1907 and the famous Bauhaus in 1919, and of Scandinavians. For this lost opportunity the influence of Morris, so beneficial in so many ways, must be held largely responsible. Through his antipathy to machinery, he and many of his followers failed to realize that machines, under skilful control, can produce good, well-designed furniture at a much lower cost than hand-made furniture. Morris was, however, obliged to use machinery for woven textiles.

CHAPTER EIGHT

Modern Trends

UNTIL 1914, when *Art Nouveau* was in its final phase, England was still a source of inspiration abroad, and chairs by Arts and Crafts designers, particularly Gimson's, were considered among the most interesting in Europe. Windsor chairs, too, produced in large numbers at High Wycombe, upheld the inherently sound and simple traditions of English chair design. But the folly of indiscriminate machine production was glaringly revealed in the post-war furnishing boom of the 1920s. To meet the demands of the mass market, manufacturers, exactly as the Morris school had feared, produced imitations of hand-made furniture, much of it even in revived antique styles. Chairs in mock-Tudor and Stuart versions, of indifferent design, construction and materials, sometimes complete with 'bulbs' or spiral turning, were turned out in their thousands at the very time when able designers abroad were using the machine to make chairs of excellent design for the ordinary market.

This confusion between tradition and imitation has been the great error of 20th-century English furniture manufacturers. The true English tradition in chair design has been to use the most suitable materials and techniques in a forthright, well-defined manner, and this approach is as evident with the rural craftsman and his local woods as with the fashionable maker and his vastly greater resources. While Gimson, therefore, worthily maintained this tradition in hand-made furniture, contemporary manufacturers who used the machine and modern materials merely to copy chairs of a former age were completely disregarding it.

But one outstanding firm, alive to the implications of the Modern Movement, emerged in the early decades of the century. Ambrose Heal (1872–1959) was a product of the Arts and Crafts Movement and won a silver medal for his bedroom suite at the Paris Exhibition of 1900. Of greater historical importance than his exhibition

87. Three varieties of
mahogany dining-chair
made by Heal & Son,
c. 1905.

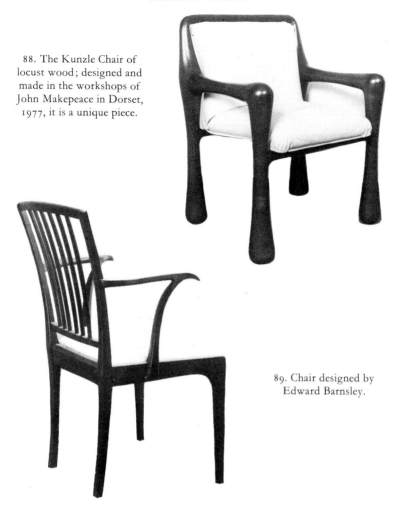

88. The Kunzle Chair of locust wood; designed and made in the workshops of John Makepeace in Dorset, 1977, it is a unique piece.

89. Chair designed by Edward Barnsley.

work, however, was the commercial production by his famous firm in Tottenham Court Road of simple, well-designed and relatively cheap furniture, beginning with the first catalogue of Heal's *Plain Oak Furniture* in 1898. His chairs were of unpolished and unstained wood and included a popular lattice-back type. He became a pioneer in the design of excellent furniture for machine production, proving himself as gifted commercially as he was technically (*illus. 87*).

The late 1920s saw some remarkable innovations in chair design

90. Sycamore dining-room chair
with leather cushion by Alan
Peters, 1978; the back and seat
slats of ash are flexible.

abroad, beginning in 1925 with the first cantilever chair in tubular steel by Marcel Breuer of the Bauhaus; then in 1929 came the laminated birch chair by Alvar Aalto, the Finnish architect, followed by the celebrated Barcelona chair in solid stainless steel by Mies van der Rohe, also of the Bauhaus. Since 1945 Danish chair design has attracted wide attention. One famous chair designed by Hans Wegner in 1949 is made by machine, but requires finishing by hand – an interesting development.

In England at this time a growing number of small shops continued to make good furniture mainly by hand, under the direction of designers like Peter Waals, formerly Gimson's foreman, and Edward Barnsley, son of Sidney Barnsley, Gimson's colleague. The latter's workshop at Petersfield is today distinguished for its beautiful furniture in the true Morris-Gimson succession

91. Graham Stewart's design for 'Serenade' was inspired by petal formations. The beech veneered frame and lap-over cushions are complemented by the use of rattan; made by Collins and Hayes.

(*illus. 89*). Some larger firms also employed well-known foreign designers, but most manufacturers were content with a depressingly low standard.

A very important exception is Sir Gordon Russell (b. 1892) who, like Heal, was reared in the Arts and Crafts Movement and in the 1920s followed directly in Gimson's footsteps with his ladder-back turned chairs with rush seats. In the 1930s he also took the significant step into machine production and his factory-made furniture at Broadway matches the best of foreign design while remaining truly English in inspiration. His commercial success has had considerable influence on contemporary taste. Heal and Russell thus emerge as two major figures, fostering the great

92. Armchair with laminated framework of resin-bonded beech veneers, dyed hide arms, back and seat of steel mesh, and fabric-covered foam cushions. Designed by Nicholas Frewing and made by Race Furniture, it won the Design Centre Award for 1966.

inheritance of hand-craft, at the same time bringing England into the full flow of the Modern Movement.

Russell was one of the designers responsible for the excellent scheme of 'utility' furniture, of standard specification and design, which was introduced by the government during the Second World War to meet the timber shortage. Some fine chairs, of good proportions and clean lines, were made. It took time, however, to educate the public, for the immediate post-war years saw manufacturers revert to eye-catching mannerisms which, they insisted, sold more easily. But there are positive signs today that higher standards of design are being both sought and reached. There may be the end in sight to what W. R. Lethaby described in 1915 (*Form in Civilization*, 1922), when English leadership in furniture was lost, as 'timid reaction and the re-emergence of the catalogued "styles"'.

93. This foam-upholstered armchair by Brian Long won the 1971 Dunlopillo Design Award. The shell is of glass-reinforced plastic; the foam is covered in polyurethane fabric.

Glossary of Chairs

Abbotsford chair A tall chair with spiral-turned uprights in the Victorian version of 'Elizabethan'; of heavy, dark wood, usually oak. Inspired by the novels of Sir Walter Scott and named after his house at Abbotsford.

'arc-back' A chair of classical design of *c*. 1800, the time of the revival of the Greek *klismos*. The back sometimes had a broad concave yoke at shoulder level, although a type of 'scroll-back' was more usual.

back chair In the 17th century this was another term for an elbow chair or a chair with arms.

back stool (or 'farthingale chair') This was the first chair without arms, introduced after 1550. It developed owing to a change in the dining arrangements, whereby the family now had its own dining-room. Now stools with backs were used, the back legs being continued into uprights, which were linked by one or two rails or a panel and were tilted slightly backwards. Although back stools were what we would now call single chairs, they were called stools to preserve the conventionalities of rank within the household. A plainer type of *c*. 1650 had a seat and back covered with leather which was tacked on with rows of brass nails. Ince and Mayhew illustrated two 'back stool chairs' in the *Universal System* of 1759–62. The term 'back stool' was still occasionally used in the latter half of the 18th century. *See* Yorkshire and Derbyshire chair.

balloon-back A modern term for the Victorian round curved back, one result of the Victorians' search for comfort. The style was anticipated by the sweep-back chairs of *c*. 1840. The yoke rail of the Grecian type and the 'scroll-back' of Louis XIV were rounded off as the next step. By about 1850 the very popular complete balloon-back had appeared with cabriole legs for the drawing-room and straight legs for the dining-room.

bamboo chair The light, jointed stems of some treelike tropical reeds were used in their natural colour, a creamy yellow, for chairs in the Chinese taste from the 18th century. Later they were painted. Bamboo was sometimes imitated by turning beech in the same form and painting it to look like bamboo, although other colours were occasionally used. The vogue for bamboo furniture continued until Victorian times.

'bended'-back (or fiddle-back) A type of chair with the baluster splat curved for comfort at shoulder level below a centrally dipping crest-rail. Used on curvilinear chairs.

bentwood chair A cheap, light and comfortable chair of simple design. It was made from inexpensive woods, like beech, which were bent under pressure with heat and moisture. The Austrian firm of Thonet was the first to use steam

94. Balloon-back drawing-room chair in mahogany of *c.* 1860 with cabriole legs.

95. *Bergère*-type armchair of *c.* 1810; it is japanned black and gold with cane sides and seat.

power and standardised designs for the mass production of these chairs. At first they were made of veneers bent in moulds with heat, and later of solid beech, often stained black. Bentwood chairs rivalled the Windsors in popularity in the Victorian period.

bergère A winged armchair introduced from France *c.* 1725. The backs, arms and sides of this deep, low-backed chair were either caned or upholstered or a combination of both, and cushioned.

bow-back chair *See* hoop-back.

cabriole chair A late Georgian term for a chair with a stuffed back, confusing because of the more usual use of the word in reference to the cabriole leg. Hepplewhite referred to the cabriole chair in the *Guide* of 1788.

cane chair The first new type of chair to appear after the Restoration, although familiar in Holland and France for some time. The seat and back were filled with cane-work made of a large coarse mesh of split rattans, from a kind of palm grown in the Far East and imported by the East India Company. The early chairs had flat, curved arms. The main decoration was the spiral turning of the uprights, legs and stretchers, which were mortised and tenoned. Sometimes shallow herring-bone stamping decorated the back frame and the seat rail.

They were usually made in sets of two armchairs and six or more single chairs. When they became fashionable about the middle of Charles II's reign, much of their good proportion was lost. Backs became higher and the cresting deeper; a broad, flat stretcher replaced the turned front rail, all covered with lavish carving, at first on solid ground and later pierced. The arms, now of round or oval section, curved downwards in the centre and scrolled over the supports. Elongated scrolls were used for the arm supports and front legs. Cane chairs remained popular during the reign of William and Mary, but became more subdued. Vertical lines were favoured and some very tall chairs were made; the spiral and turned uprights were replaced by balusters turned in graceful forms and the cane-work was of a very fine mesh.

caquetoire Appearing before 1550, it was a light type of panel-back, supposedly intended as a conversation chair. It generally had a tall, narrow, rectangular back often decorated with carving. By *c.* 1600 the panels beneath the seat and arms had been discarded, allowing the arms to curve to support the elbow and scroll beyond the supports; the arm supports and front legs might be turned.

chair-table A useful piece of furniture in which the back of the chair, often covered with carved decoration, swings forward on a pivot to form a table. Made from Romano-British and late medieval times to the 18th century, being particularly popular in the 17th century (*illus. 18*).

chair of state (or estate) A throne-like chair which figures prominently in medieval records for persons of the highest rank. It is often shown as a magnificent towering structure surmounted by a canopy of wainscot or of costly material. It stood on a dais against the wall with a 'dosser' at the back and a 'banker' on the seat, both of rich fabric. Some had cases of leather for travelling. The most famous example is the Coronation Chair in Westminster Abbey, although much changed.

'chamber' chair *See* sweep-back.

chamber horse A seat-like device used for exercising in the second half of the 18th century. The leather-covered seat had a concertina effect due to the springs inside, which allowed it to go up and down almost as if one were on horseback. Sometimes there was a footboard and a drawer under the seat.

cock-fighting chair *See* library chair.

comb-back The earliest type of Windsor, named after the shaped top rail supported on sticks. Usually made of elm, it incorporates splats, cabriole legs (often of a clumsy appearance), with pad feet and stretchers. On armchairs a horizontal hoop formed a semicircle across the back and along to the front as arm supports. The back sticks passed through this hoop which was supported at the sides by sticks from the seat. All members were set at an angle, the legs and arm supports being splayed and the sticks raked outwards. From the 1750s the side stretchers were sometimes united by a curved stretcher. For extra strength two stays forming a brace might be found fixed from the top of the back to a small platform or bob-tail projecting from the rear of the seat. Decoration was confined to turning or the piercing of the splat with motifs inspired by fashionable decoration. Some fine examples made after 1750 had, instead of sticks in the back, a series of splats pierced with Gothic tracery. Later in the century the wheel motif and the Prince of Wales's feathers motif were also found. Sometimes made in mahogany for the big houses.

compass chair With rounded seat, introduced in the early 18th century.

conversation chair Has a deep upholstered seat and a padded top rail upon which the sitter, facing backwards, could rest his arms. Sheraton illustrated this chair in his *Drawing-Book*, 1791–4.

curricle In the Regency period, a tub-shaped chair in the classical style, named after a carriage by Sheraton in his *Cabinet Dictionary* of 1803.

curule Shaped like a camp stool with crossed front and back legs, usually braced by one or more stretchers, it was made to be folded up, so as to be convenient for travel. The framework was completely covered with rich materials and loose squab cushions resting on webbing. It was used in Roman Britain, and by the end of the medieval period was being made by the coffer-makers.

'devotional' chair *See prie-dieu.*

'Egyptian' chair Such chairs were made during a short-lived attempt to integrate Egyptian motifs into furniture design, of which Thomas Hope was the chief exponent in England. Popular versions appeared after 1798, the year Napoleon's Egyptian campaign was cut short by Nelson's victory at the Nile;

96. 'Egyptian' armchair of *c*. 1805; of ebonised wood it is gilded, with reeded crossed front supports of 'curule' type; Egyptian figures form the arm supports.

97. (*Right*) 'Etruscan' armchair, gilded, of *c*. 1800.

the Egyptian revival became a craze in England. From 1802 Europe had access to accurate archaeological data of Egyptian antiquities, which further stimulated interest. Favourite motifs for chairs included the sphinx, the lotus leaf and scarabs. There were many imitations in flimsy materials at this time. George Smith exploited Egyptian motifs in his *Household Furniture* of 1808. Egyptian motifs were revived in the late Victorian period, e.g. Liberty's 'Thebes stool' of 1884.

elbow chair A 17th-century term to distinguish a chair with arms from one without. It can be another term for armchair.

'Etruscan' chair This style of chair first appeared in the neo-classical period, from *c*.1760. The fine gilt armchairs were influenced by French 'Etruscan' types, which were, in reality, derived from Greek vase painting. The Adam brothers claimed to have introduced this style, which became so popular that an 'Etruscan Room' was occasionally introduced into the big houses. These chairs had strongly curved rear legs, scrolled uprights and arm supports, and straight or curved front legs. The arms, where the downward sweep is balanced by the inward curve of the supports, represent one of the most elegant developments of the time. Another feature, common by 1805, was an even bolder scroll downwards and inwards coming to rest on the side rails of the seat. The vogue was further spread by the publication in 1766 of *Antiquités Etrusques, Grecques et Romaines*, the plates of Sir William Hamilton's collection.

'fancy chair' *See* sweep-back.

'farthingale chair' In Elizabethan times a type of upholstered chair made without arms; so named later because of the belief that these chairs were designed to accommodate a lady's farthingale, a wide skirt enlarged at the hips by metal hoops. *See* back stool.

fiddle-back *See* 'bended'-back.

'fly' chair A light and elegant style of chair in the French taste, suitable for a lady's apartment in the early Victorian period. It had a carved and gilded back of curvilinear form, and cabriole legs.

folding chair Introduced after 1550 as an improved and lighter version of the back stool, which had immediately preceded it as a new and distinctive type of chair. Closely resembling Italian models, the arms were shaped to support the elbows and were hinged by a wooden rod passing through the top of the front legs and the sides of the seat. Typical decorations for the back were carved round arches, each enclosing a lozenge. It was sometimes called a 'Glastonbury' chair after an example in Shaw's *Specimens*, in which it is described as 'the Abbot's chair, Glastonbury' and incorrectly dated to the reign of Henry VIII.

garden chair Chairs designed specifically for the garden were included in the 1762 edition of Chippendale's *Director*; as with the other chairs in this pattern book, they represented the English version of the rococo.

'Glastonbury' chair *See* folding chair.

gondola chair (or spoon-back) A distinct chair type of the late Georgian period with continuous upholstered back and seat.

gossip's chair *See caquetoire*

hall chair Introduced into the big houses of early Georgian England, these

98. Ladder-back chair in ash with rush seat, designed and made by Ernest Gimson, *c.* 1890s. Victoria and Albert Museum, London.

99. Hall chair of *c.* 1750; the back of this mahogany chair is carved with lion mask and drapery.

chairs were designed to be used in the entrance hall and passageways for the convenience of servants and tradesmen. They were therefore never upholstered, being made of mahogany with solid backs and seats, usually dished. From the 1760s sets of 12, 18 and even 36 were made. To impress important visitors, the strong, plain design was often embellished with a painted crest, marquetry or carving, perhaps with the mask and drapery motifs. Hall chairs usually had columnar or straight turned legs. In the second half of the 18th century an oval-, round- or vase-shaped back was preferred, joined to the seat by a narrow back rail. The back might be pierced to form a pattern of scrolling loops. Hall chairs were illustrated in Hepplewhite's *Guide* of 1788 and Sheraton included them in *The Cabinet Dictionary* of 1803.

heart-back A type of neo-classical chair, usually of mahogany, with, as the name implies, a heart-shaped back. Along with the lyre-back and shield-back, it gave the chairs of this period an elegant lightness.

hoop-back (or bow-back) One variety of the enormously popular Windsor, the hoop-back has a curved top rail into which the sticks were socketed. Splats are sometimes used with, or in place of, the sticks, and are sometimes pierced with tracery. The arms continue round the back to form a single back rail. The hoop-back came into use *c.*1750 and, although more familiar, never superseded the comb-back.

iron chair Made in cast iron and popular for the garden in the 19th century.

joined (or 'joyned') chair *See* panel-back.

klismos A Greek chair apparently based on a simple type of throne which was most probably used in Roman Britain; it had forward-curving front sabre legs and opposing rear legs which swept upwards into the back to a curved horizontal back board. This style was revived during the Regency period when it was skilfully interpreted and had a revolutionary effect on chair design; the continuous curve of the uprights and rear legs balanced the concave front legs.

ladder-back (or slat-back) A type of country chair with high uprights joined by horizontal slats. It dates from medieval times when there was a type of ladder-back which had 'rungs' of turned spindles. Later the style varied from area to area, such as the Lancashire ladder-back. In the Chippendale period the turned ladder-back became a fashionable mahogany piece, with refinements. It was revived again by Ernest Gimson of the 'Cotswold School' who designed elegant rush-seated ladder-backs in the 1890s.

lath-back A type of Windsor used extensively as a kitchen chair from *c.*1860. It had a saddle seat and a plain slat-like top rail which were attached to each other by four or five plain outward-curving horizontal slats and two side rails. The legs had some turning; the front and back legs were joined by stretchers.

lattice-work back A chair back carved with a lattice-like see-through pattern, with the strips crossing diagonally. Lattice-work backs were used in the Georgian period for some chairs in the Chinese taste. Ambrose Heal also designed a popular chair of this type.

'library chair' A chair type introduced when the Palladian houses of early Georgian England were being built, usually with a library instead of a long gallery. It was made with padded arms and back on which the sitter, astride the chair facing the rear, could rest his arms. A small desk for reading and writing was also attached to the back for his use. Sometimes called a 'cock-fighting' chair; while this may possibly have been so, it is unlikely. Its main function was in the library.

'love seat' A modern term for a type of chair dating from the early 18th century; it describes a large broad chair, wide enough for two people and similar to a settee.

lyre-back A light and attractive neo-classical chair with a back in a lyre-shape; it is decorated with finely carved or inlaid classical ornaments, all carefully related to the structural design of the chair. The design originated with Robert Adam and was one of the most important English contributions to European chair design.

Mendlesham or Suffolk chair A distinct type of Windsor, really the East Anglian variety. It has a seat and legs like the Windsor with a back of square or rectangular shape, a straight top rail, vertical spindles, turned balls in the space between the top and a cross rail, and a narrow vertical splat. Said to have first been made by Daniel Day of Mendlesham in Suffolk in the late 18th century.

'Moorish' chair One of several styles popular during the later Victorian

100. Library or reading chair in walnut of *c.* 1725; upholstered in leather, it has an adjustable board, hinged trays, candle-holders below the arms and a drawer below the seat.

period. 'Moorish' chairs, with much interlaced patterning in the backs, were made, notably by Liberty's, for 'Moorish' smoking rooms.

Morris chair An extremely popular style of easy chair, both in England and the United States, produced by William Morris's firm and made from *c.* 1866. An upholstered long-seated easy chair with an adjustable back, it was far lighter than most contemporary easy chairs, and was one of the less expensive types produced by Morris. The firm also produced the famous Sussex chairs, a light chair painted dark green with rush seat copied from an old country type.

'mortuary' chair A carved human head with a pointed beard appears in the centre of the arch of some Yorkshire and Derbyshire chairs. It is supposed that this commemorates Charles I and reflects the royalist sympathies of northern England after his execution. Although possible, there is no contemporary authority for this name.

nursing chair In country furniture, a chair or rocking chair without arms. In Victorian times some handsome walnut nursing chairs were made.

oval-back One of Adam's neo-classical chair designs closely following French styles. The carved and gilded chair had an oval back, sometimes supported by winged sphinxes. Adam's oval-back ranks as one of the most graceful in the history of chair-making.

page's chair *See* porter's chair.

panel-back Made from the 15th to early 17th centuries, it was a box-like joined chair, probably derived from the chest, with panelled back, sides and seat, without legs and with arms provided by the flat rails of the side panels. The top panel at the back might be covered with Renaissance decoration. At first the panels were decorated with carved Gothic tracery and linen-fold carving. The panel-back was a direct result of the joiners applying the constructional technique of the panel and frame to chair-making. The framework of vertical stiles and horizontal rails was secured by mortise and tenon joints. The panel, tapered on all sides, fitted into grooves on the inside of the frame and was allowed sufficient movement to prevent warping. Many Elizabethan panel-backs were decorated with inlay and strapwork. A light type appeared *c.* 1550, the *caquetoire*. *See caquetoire.*

papier mâché chair A vogue for this type began when the chief makers, Jennens and Bettridge of Birmingham (whose chairs are frequently stamped with their names), used papier mâché, usually on a framework of wood or metal, for a wide range of furniture including chairs in the 1820s. The chair shape was built up, then smoothed and finally japanned black. Decoration was in the form of painted flowers or scenes in natural colours, sometimes embellished with bronze powder ornament, gilding or pearl-shell inlay. Although sometimes derided, papier mâché was most often used with skill and understanding, resulting in light and attractive chairs. Its plastic qualities were excellently used for the moulded backs of *bergère* chairs. In the early Victorian period some were made in the 'Elizabethan' style.

porter's (or page's or watchman's) chair An 18th-century chair usually made of leather with wings and a high arched top to keep out the draughts in the halls of town and country houses. Provided for a man-servant, who perhaps waited to open the door.

prie-dieu (or 'devotional', or 'vesper') A chair with a tall upholstered back, low seat and short legs, an original early Victorian contribution to English chair design. Some chairs had elaborate turned uprights and legs derived from late Stuart models, and were intended for the drawing-room. A specifically devotional type with a T-shaped back and padded top-rest for family prayers was popular around the mid century.

Queen Anne chair A walnut chair with a back of curvilinear outline enclosing a central splat, itself pierced and carved with foliated ornament; the cabriole front legs were united by a stretcher. At first the uprights were only slightly curved, but they gradually acquired a more pronounced hoop form relieved by a small angle at the hips. The central splat, which was attached to the back rail of the seat by a moulded 'shoe' was now solid. It was 'bended' at shoulder level, for comfort, and shaped into various vase or fiddle forms. The style was first inspired by the designs of Daniel Marot, a French Huguenot living in Holland, who entered the service of William III. The curvilinear chair outlasted the reign of Queen Anne (1702–14).

reading and writing chair *See* library chair, writing chair.

'ribband-back' The splat of a mahogany chair was carved to represent inter-woven silk ribbons expressing the more extravagant rococo taste. First

102. 'Smoker's bow' type Windsor chair *c.* 1860

101. Papier mâché chair of *c.* 1860 decorated with polychrome and inlaid with mother-of-pearl. Victoria and Albert Museum, London.

illustrated by Thomas Chippendale in his *Director* of 1754, continuing to the 1770s–80s.

rococo chair A typical example (*c.* 1750–65) had pierced and interlaced splats with carved scrollwork in varied light and fanciful forms which could only be executed in mahogany; uprights gently curving outwards, top rail of 'cupid's bow' shape; front legs could be straight or tapered or of delicately carved cabriole form, usually ending on a scroll; stretchers were reintroduced on chairs with straight legs, although unnecessary structurally; the upholstery was stuffed over the rails with a brass border neatly chased, but also done with brass nails in one or two rows. The style was firmly established by Chippendale when he published his *Director*, 1754.

scoop-back *See* gondola chair.

'scroll-back' With uprights scrolling outwards and backwards, it was one of the more usual types of Regency chair.

shield-back A chair designed by Robert Adam, and others, in the neo-classical style, resulting in an elegant light appearance. These chairs were decorated with finely carved or inlaid classical ornaments, with front legs that might be fluted and decorated. It was Hepplewhite who translated this design into general use through his *Guide*, 1788.

slat-back *See* ladder-back.

'sleeping chayres' Winged chairs in the period after the Restoration, with ratchets to adjust the slope of the back; they were elaborately carved, gilded and upholstered.

'smoker's bow' A Windsor with a low back and arms forming a horizontal semicircle with the yoke rail, supported from the seat by turned spindles; it usually had splayed legs and a saddle seat. Appearing after 1825, it was sturdy, cheap and comfortable. This was the most popular and ubiquitous of all the variants of the Windsor, and was found in cottages, small houses in the suburbs, public smoking rooms and institutions.

smoker's chair Made in the late Victorian period, with a drawer below the seat for smoker's equipment.

spindle-back With a back composed of turned rods, either straight or with a slight swelling at the centre, the spindle-back was an obvious manifestation of the turner's craft. Made from local woods, it was one of a variety of country chairs made for cottages, farmhouses and inns.

spoon-back chair *See* gondola chair.

square-back A chair with a square back, accentuating the vertical lines of the chair by varied and original arrangements of bars, which are in some instances grouped into a central splat. A popular style in the Georgian period, and illustrated in Sheraton's *Drawing-Book*, 1791–4.

stick-back The back consists of stick-like spindles joining the top rail and the back of the seat; Windsors are a variety of stick-back.

Sussex chair *See* Morris chair.

sweep-back The back was formed by the continuous curve of the side and top rails, with dips at the top and side. There was a fairly narrow carved splat and the front legs were straight of columnar form. Sweep-backs were illustrated in Thomas King's *Original Designs for Chairs, etc.* of *c.*1840. The name also applied to a slender cane-seated version, which were also termed 'fancy' or 'chamber' chairs.

tall-back In the William and Mary period tall-back chairs were much favoured, with arched cresting placed above the tops of the uprights to make them even taller. Although very graceful in appearance the backward rake and the use of dowel jointing resulted in a structural weakness. More recently, Charles Rennie Mackintosh designed some famous tall-backs.

'Trafalgar' chair A type of Regency parlour chair, which first appeared shortly after 1800, became known as the 'Trafalgar' chair after the 1805 naval victory. This version had sabre front legs, of oblong section, narrower in the front than at the back, with side rails making a continuous curve with swept-back uprights, and outward-curving rear legs. The light appearance was enhanced by a cane seat on which a squab cushion was fastened from underneath, and by the simple filling, sometimes also cane, in the back. The top is either a shoulder board or a turned rail, often with rope or cable moulding, and curved for the sitter's back. Normally made of beech, painted black or bronze-green. Many variations on this theme are found.

turned or 'thrown' chair Produced by the turners on their lathes, this traditional type of chair was made from the medieval period, when it was a ladder-back with 'rungs' of turned spindles. There were several early variations. A common type had a triangular seat into which three sturdy turned posts were fixed at the corners. Near the end of the medieval period a plain type had bobbin-

103. 'Trafalgar' chair of *c.* 1810; in stained beech it has sabre front legs and rope moulding on top rail and back uprights. Victoria and Albert Museum, London.

104. Windsor chair in yew of *c.* 1760; of hoop-back form, the splats are pierced with Gothic tracery; it has cabriole legs and a curved front stretcher.

turned arms linking the front posts to a horizontal board for supporting the shoulders on the back post, and turned stretchers connecting the bottom of the three posts just above floor level. There was also a more elaborate version with a back framework built up of a variety of ornamental spindles and connected to the front posts by ringed rails; a series of spindles joined the front stretcher to the seat. This type, becoming more and more ornate, was made well into the Stuart period, in a variety of patterns. After the Restoration, the popular cane chair was decorated mainly with spiral turning of the uprights, legs and stretchers. The turning might be knob, ball, bobbin, ring, spiral or baluster.

'utility' furniture Furniture made to standard specification and design, which was introduced by the government during the Second World War in order to meet the timber shortages. Some fine chairs of good proportions were made. Sir Gordon Russell, who found commercial success with his use of machine production for chairs, was one of the designers responsible for this scheme.

'vesper' *See prie-dieu.*

'White Wycombes' Windsor chairs sold without stain or paint, mainly in the area in which they were made – High Wycombe, Buckinghamshire.

wickerwork chair The back and sides were one continuous piece of wickerwork, the shoulder-high back sloping down to form arm rests. The base was also of wickerwork on all sides, possibly of a coarser mesh. Made of plaited or woven twigs or young willow branches, these chairs were known before and during the Roman occupation, and have been made ever since.

window seat (or window stool) A neo-classical seat with ends but no back and usually upholstered, it was designed to be placed in a bay window. These seats were illustrated in Hepplewhite's *Guide* of 1794. The term can also refer to a seat built into a window; it may have a hinged top with a chest underneath.

Windsor chair A type of stick-back invented by the turners and maintaining its basic characteristics for over three centuries. The earliest was the comb-back with its shaped top rail supported on sticks. The hoop-back with its bent bow back into which the sticks are socketed came into use after 1750. Elm was usually used for the saddle seat, while beech was favoured for the sticks, legs and stretchers, and ash or yew for the bentwood features. The round turned legs were socketed into holes bored underneath the seat, and the sticks for the backs were fitted into holes bored in the top of the seat. Both types sometimes had splats and cabriole legs, the latter having pad feet and stretchers. On armchairs a horizontal hoop often formed a semicircle across the back and along to the front as arm supports. All members of a chair were set at an angle, the legs and arm supports being splayed and the sticks raked outwards. From the 1750s the side stretchers were sometimes united by a curved stretcher. For extra strength the stays forming a brace were sometimes fixed from the top of the back to a small platform or bob-tail projecting from the rear of the seat. Decoration was either in the turning or the piercing of the splat. After 1750 the splats were decorated with Gothic tracery, the wheel motif or the Prince of Wales's feathers motif. They were sometimes stained red, presumably to resemble mahogany. Windsors were made for the big houses and for palaces, usually in mahogany. The style was transplanted in the North American colonies where it took on a new life and became very popular for the same reasons that made it popular in Britain – it was light, inexpensive and of pleasing design. The basic simplicity of this design appealed to the reformist designers of the 1860s, who adapted it to their taste, the kitchen version having a broad yoke, like that of a Grecian chair, supported by sticks, spindles or lathes. *See also* Mendlesham chair; 'White Wycombes'.

writing chair An early Georgian chair having three legs at the front and one at the back; sometimes with two splats and a semicircular top rail. *See also* library chair; reading and writing chair.

X-framed chair A traditional chair from the earliest times, it has two X-frames, either at the sides braced by stretchers, or at the back and front. The back was formed by extended uprights joined by webbing as were the sides. It could easily be folded up and carried. The style became fashionable in the Tudor period.

Yorkshire and Derbyshire chair A variety of the back stool, which was made in the late 1660s. The back was filled, either with two wide, flat hoops decorated with carving and attached pendants, or with an open arcade of turned balusters between two connecting rails. A carved head with a pointed beard is sometimes found in the centre of the arched top. It takes its name from the counties in which it was made, although it was also made in Lancashire.

Index

N.B.: Page numbers in *italic* refer to illustrations where these are separated from the text. For chair types see also the Glossary, pp. 114–26.

Aalto, Alvar 110
Abbotsford chair 114
Adam style 52, *63*, 73–7
Aesthetic Movement 101
Anglo-Saxon period 12–13
apron-piece 57
'arc-back' 85
'Art Furniture'/Arts and
   Crafts 100ff
Art Nouveau 102, 104–6ff

back chair 31, 33
back stool 28–31, 36, *43*.
   See also 'farthingale'
   chair
Baillie Scott, M. H. *105*
'balloon-back' 94, *115*
bamboo chair 101
   imitation *64*, 66, 87
'banker' 17
'bar-back' 80
Barcelona chair 110
Barnsley family 104, *109*,
   110
Bauhaus 106, 110
'bended'-back 49
bentwood chair 71, 97
'*bergère*' *79*, 87, 96, *115*
Birch, William *105*
Breuer, Marcel 110
Bridgens, Richard 17
Brown, Ford Madox 99
Brown, Richard 88
Burges, W. 100

Cabinet Dictionary 22, 82, 83
cabriole chair/leg 48–51ff
cane chair 38ff, *43*, 78, 82,
   85–7
'*caquetoire*' 27, 28
chair of (e)state 9–11, 16–19,
   22, 33
chair-table *35*
chaise longue 82
Chambers, Sir William 74
Chinese style 49, 62–5, 66,
   84, 87
Chippendale style 21, 52,
   61–8, 74–5
church chairs 14–19
'claw and ball' 49–50, 54–7
cock-fighting chair 60–61

Collcutt, T. E. 100
Collinson & Lock of
   London 100
'comb-back' 70–72
'*confidante*' 80, 98
conversation chair 82, 98
Coronation Chair *15*, 17–19
'Cotswold School' 104ff
couch. *See* day bed, *etc.*
'country' chairs 68–70
'curricle' 87
'curule' 11, 87

Day, Daniel 73
day-bed/couch 47, 59, 87
'*Director*' (Chippendale)
   62ff, 70, 73
'dormante' furniture 13
'*Drawing-Book*' (Sheraton)
   79, 80–82
'*duchesse*' 80
Dutch. *See* Flemish

Eastlake style 97, 99–100
Edwardian period 103ff
Egyptian style 9, 83, 84, 87,
   117
elbow chair 20, 31, 72
'Elizabethan' (19th-century)
   88–92; *cf* Tudor
Etruscan style 84, 87, *117*

faldstool 20
'farthingale chair' 36, *See
   also* back stool
Flanders/Flemish/Dutch 22,
   23ff, 41, 42, 48
'fly' chair 91
folding chair 19, 31, 32, 33
French influence 44, 62ff
'French scroll' 65, 67, 77
Frewing, Nicholas *112*

garden chair 65
Georgian period 52–87
gesso 57–8
gilt 57ff, 82, 85–7, 91, 96
Gimson, Ernest 21, 104,
   107, 110
'Glastonbury' chair 31, *34*.
   See also folding chair
Godwin, E. W. 100–*101*

gondola chair 87
'Gothic' 84–5, 92–3, 99–100
'Gothick' 62–5, 67
Goudin *le jeune* 67
Grecian style 9, 83, 87,
   89–91
Guide (Hepplewhite) 76–80
guilloche 28, 32

hall chair 61, 65, 80, *119*
Hardwick, Philip 90
Heal, Ambrose 107–9,
   111–12
heart-back 76–7
Hepplewhite style 52, 73ff,
   76–80
Holland, Henry 83
hoop-back 71–2, *125*
Hope, Thomas 84

Ince, W. and Mayhew, J.
   31, 65
inlay 28–9, 95–6

Jacobean. *See* Stuart, early
Japanese style 100–101
japanning 43, 45, 51, 59, 66,
   78ff, 95–6
Jennens & Bettridge of
   Birmingham 96
joined/joyned chair. *See*
   panel-back

Kent, William 58–9, 68
King, Thomas 89–92, 94
klismos 9–11, 84, 90
'knurl foot' 65
Kunzle chair *109*

ladder-back 20–21, 70, *119*
lath-back 96
lattice-back *64*, 66, 81, 109
'library' chair 59–61, *121*.
   See also writing chair
Linnel, John 66, 75
'lion-period' 54–7ff
Long, Brian *113*
'love-seat' 47–8
lyre-back 75–6

Mackintosh, C. R. *103*, 106
Mackmurdo, A. H. 101–2

mahogany 53–4ff
imitation 73
Makepeace, John 109
Manwaring, Robert 65
Marot, Daniel 48
marquetry 37, 51
medieval period 14–22
Mendlesham chair 73
modern period 107–13
monopodia 85–7
Morris chair 99–101, 104
Morris, William 13, 99–104, 110
'mortuary' chair 36

neo-classical style 73ff

ottoman 98
oval-back 75–7, 80

panel-back 21–2, 25–8, 70
papier mâché chair 93, 96, 123
parcel-gilt 57, 59
patera 76–7
Peters, Alan 110
pouffe 98
prie-dieu 96, 98
Prince of Wales's feathers 77–8
Pugin, A. W. N. 92–3

Queen Anne chair 48–51

'railing'. See lattice-back
reeding 81–2
Regency style 82–7
'ribband-back' 65
rococo 61–8, 90
Roman style 9–11, 83
Russell, Sir Gordon 111

sabre/scimitar leg 9, 85
Salvin, Anthony 92
scroll-back 85, 91
'serpentine line' 68, 70
settee 47, 75, 79, 80, 82, 86–7
Shaw, Henry 17, 19, 31, 89
Sheraton style 22, 52, 79, 80–82ff
shield-back 76ff
side chair 42
'sleeping chair' 44–5, 46
Smith, George 84, 87, 89, 91
'smoker's bow' 96, 123
'sociable' 98
sofa 86–7
solium 11
Specimens of Ancient Furniture 17, 19, 31, 89
spindle-back 70, 96
square-back 78–81, 104
Stewart, Graham 111
stick-back 70, 96
stool 11, 13, 22
    18th-century 67, 77, 80
    folding 11, 20 44
    footstool 31, 33, 47
    joined/joint 26, 33
    19th-century 86–7, 97
    Stuart 33, 40, 47
    See also back stool
strapwork 28–9, 62
Stuart, James 74
Stuart period 31, 51
Suffolk chair. See Mendlesham
Sussex chair 99, 101
sweep-back 92, 94

Talbert, B. J. 100
tall-back 42, 91–2, 106

'tête-à-tête' 98
Thomson, P. 92
Thonet, Michael 97
thrown chair. See turned
'Trafalgar' chair 85–7, 125
Tudor period 23–32ff
'Turkey work' 26–8
turned chair 20–21, 24, 31, 38–9, 70

United States of America 21, 52, 63, 73
'utility' furniture 112, 125

Van der Rohe, Mies 110
vase-shaped back 49
Victorian period 88–98, 99ff
Voysey, C. F. A. 104

Waals, Peter 110
watchman's chair. See porter's
Webb, Philip 99
Wegner, Hans 110
Whitaker, Henry 89–90
White Wycombe 73
wickerwork chair 10–11, 31
window seat/stool 80
Windsor chair 21, 70–73, 96–7, 107. See also hoop-back, 'smoker's bow'
winged chair 45, 51, 53, 80
Wood, Henry 92
writing chair 59–60

X-frame chair (Frontispiece), 18–19, 25, 31–2, 33, 86–7

'Yorkshire and Derbyshire' chair 33, 36

ACKNOWLEDGMENTS

N.B.: Numbers refer to illustration numbers.

Illustration number 3 is reproduced by permission of the Dean and Chapter of Westminster; illustration number 5 by permission of the Dean and Chapter of Winchester Cathedral and the Frontispiece by permission of the Dean and Chapter of York.

Photographs: Norman Adams Ltd, London 58; Edward Barnsley 89; Cooper-Bridgeman Library, London 44, 78; Country Life, London 4, 104; Dunlop Ltd, London 93; Hamlyn Group Picture Library 31, 52, 77, 84, 99; Heal and Son, London 87; Robert Hosking, London 94, 102; Hotspur, London 36, 41, 42, 45, 47, 50, 62, 100; Angelo Hornak, London Frontispiece; H. W. Keil Ltd, Broadway 6, 13, 22, 34; John Makepeace Ltd, Beaminster 88; Mallet and Son, London 23, 30, 32, 48, 64; William Morris Gallery, Walthamstow 83; The National Magazine Company, London 91; The National Trust, London 14, 15, 18, 24, 26, 33, 54; Nordenfjeldske Kunstindustrimuseum, Trondheim 86; Alan Peters, Cullompton 90; Pitkin Pictorials, London 5; Phillips of Hitchin 27, 28, 38, 43, 46, 51, 55, 61; Public Records Office, London 19; Race Furniture 92; Roman Baths Museum, Bath 1; Royal Society of Arts, London 53; Temple Williams Ltd 39, 49, 59, 60, 63, 65, 67, 68, 69, 95, 96, 97; Victoria and Albert Museum, London 2, 9, 16, 17, 21, 29, 44, 66, 75, 76, 79, 81, 82, 85, 98, 101, 103; J. Barbee Winston, New Orleans 35; S. W. Wolsey Ltd, London 8, 10, 11, 20, 25.